Karate

空手入門書

空手入門書

Karate

A step-by-step guide to Shotokan karate

Kevin Healy

FIFTH DAN JKA

Photography by Laura Knox

CB

CONTEMPORARY BOOKS

To Callum, my teacher

PLEASE NOTE
The author, publisher and packager cannot accept any responsibility for injury resulting from the practice of any of the principles and techniques set out in this book. If you are in any doubt about any aspect of your condition, please refer to a medical professional.

First published in the United Kingdom in 2000 by Time-Life UK,
Brettenham House, Lancaster Place, London WC2E 7TL
This edition is published by arrangement with Eddison Sadd Editions Limited
First published in the United States in 2000 by Contemporary Books
A division of NTC/Contemporary Publishing Group, Inc.
4255 West Touhy Avenue, Lincolnwood (Chicago), Illinois 60712–1975 U.S.A.

ace
05/01

International Standard Book Number: 0-8092-9780-9

18 17 16 15 14 13 12 11 10 9 8 7 6 5 4 3 2 1

Edited, designed, and produced by Eddison Sadd Editions Limited

Contents

はじめに

Part One
Beginning the Journey

When I was first approached to write a karate book, my first thought was how best could I put down on paper a guide for those new to the art? I was concerned because karate is a living thing, and many books I have read fail to bring it to life. Karate must be practised, and only through practice do you come to meet the questions it asks of the mind and spirit.

I decided to read a book I had read as a youth almost twenty years ago: *Karate-Do: My Way of Life* by Gichin Funakoshi, the founder of modern karate. As I read through this book many lost memories returned to me, reminding me what it had been like to be a young boy new to the art. I determined then that the most important thing I could say is that karate is a lifelong endeavour with many highs and lows – a journey that never ends, but a journey well worth taking. If you decide to begin this journey, I welcome you to the practice of karate. It will change your life.

'Even a journey of a thousand miles must start with the first step.'

はじめに

Mind, Body and Spirit

My first taste of karate was on a summer's evening in 1979. The local community centre in the area where I lived was a run-down wreck of a place used by the local scouts and girl guides – not a place frequented by the lads from the local estates! As I passed by on that evening, my attention was drawn to screams and shouts followed by total silence, then more of the same. Being young and nosy, I investigated.

What I saw as I entered was something that would change the rest of my life: line after line of men and women, all wearing white suits and a variety of coloured belts, and all moving as one up and down the tiny hall, responding to the commands of the man at the front wearing a black belt. It was a hot night and the floor was covered in sweat, and condensation hung to the walls. The people looked exhausted but none flagged, none sat down to rest, none left. I was mesmerized. When the fighting started, it was ferocious, with no quarter asked or given. Looking back it seemed brutal: it was, but for good reason. I was soon to learn that karate is a test – a challenge thrown down against the mind, the body and the spirit, and the only one who can ever beat you is yourself.

Ken Healy

はじめに

The Evolution of Karate

The word *karate* itself derives from a combination of two simple parts: *kara* meaning 'empty', and *te* meaning 'hand' – hence, art of the empty hand. Why, then, the need for empty-hand fighting?

The islands of Okinawa – rich in their own martial traditions – became a prefecture of Japan, and as a result a law was passed banning the possession of all weapons. This was intended to reduce the threat of revolt. The Okinawans, however, turned this to their advantage by adapting their own indigenous arts with those that had filtered to the island from mainland China. The art that we know today was taking its first formative steps.

In 1922 Gichin Funakoshi, the founder of modern karate, was invited to mainland Japan from Okinawa to give a karate demonstration at a traditional martial arts exhibition. Funakoshi, a teacher and karate master (*Sensei*), learned his art on the island. His display was so well received by the Japanese public that he consequently decided to remain in Japan and teach his art. Soon Funakoshi had many students, and a *dojo* –

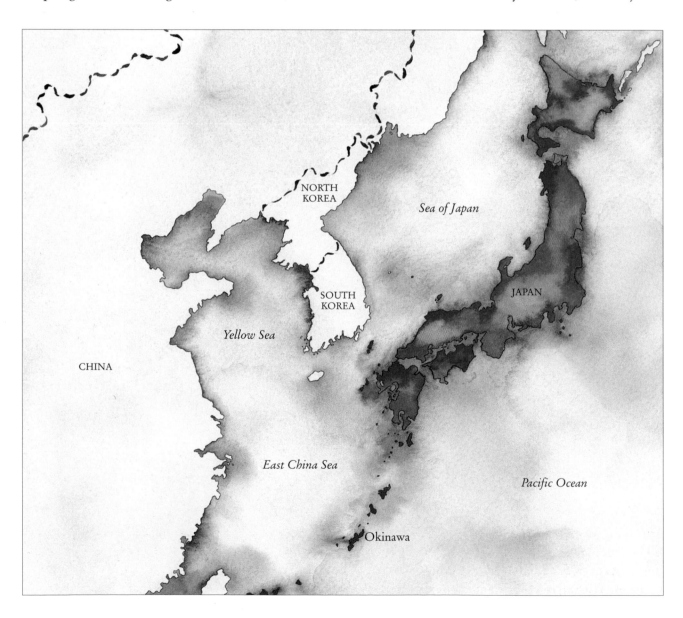

training hall – was built. This building became known as the *Shotokan*. *Shoto* was Funakoshi's pen name, and *kan* means 'training place'. The name 'Shotokan' took off, and soon Funakoshi's followers were known as those who practised Shotokan karate.

This, for me, sums up the beauty of Shotokan karate. Nothing is superfluous – from its name, which is direct and to the point, to the type of training, which is hard, demanding and also to the point. It is the most widespread style of karate practised around the world today, and one which I have been practising myself for over twenty years.

THE SPREAD OF KARATE

With karate's success, more teachers followed and other schools of karate were set up, each instructor teaching more or less along the same lines as Funakoshi but with slight variations in emphasis. At the end of the second world war and the Allied occupation of Japan, Westerners for the first time had a taste of karate. This led to karate filtering back to the USA and Europe, and soon Japanese masters from the Japan Karate Association (JKA) were being invited to the West to spread the word, much as Funakoshi did back in the 1920s.

Westerners fell in love with this new deadly art – the media, especially, falling for its mystique. In the early 1960s two karate masters arrived in Great Britain to teach. Senseis Enoeda and Kanazawa, still teaching and training today, were probably the most important catalysts in karate's development in the West. Between them, these two masters taught the very first generation of British *karate-ka* (people who practise karate) to become black belts, many of whom are now masters of karate in their own right.

KARATE TODAY

Today, there are countless karate styles and hundreds of associations and governing bodies. Over the last thirty years karate has fragmented

again and again, and these days a new student is likely to be mystified by the sheer number of clubs and styles on offer. I can only speak from personal experience, but having trained with karate-ka from every recognized style, I know that there is no 'best' or 'worst', but I also know that Shotokan karate – even after twenty years – is challenging, rewarding and a match for any of them.

ABOUT THIS BOOK

No matter how good a publication is, or how much detailed knowledge it contains, it cannot and should not act as a substitute for actual training. This training should take place in a class environment, giving the student the opportunity to encounter all kinds of characters and situations.

This book should be used to help supplement your training, and to assist you if you have a query or are struggling with a concept. Each movement is explained in great detail and shown from different angles, so if, at the end of a class, you are unsure of a point, look it up and work on it at home. There is nothing an instructor likes better than a keen student who goes away and does some 'home work'. Take, for example, the great story of a young Sensei Kanazawa who, after the rigours of six hours' training a day at the JKA headquarters, went home to his room and practised further on his weak points in front of the mirror. This dedication helped make him one of the finest karate-ka of his generation.

The words and thoughts that follow are my own, formulated after twenty years' involvement in the art. I hope I have trained and taught enough to pass on some knowledge that might inspire those new to the way. My hope is that you will study your karate deeply and, in doing so, discover that it is truly an art.

Why Choose Karate?

Leisure time has never been so important as it is in society today. Every sport imaginable is on offer to the general public. So why choose a discipline like karate over, say, mountain biking, rock climbing or running marathons? There is no set answer. Each person who is attracted to the art has their own agenda, but karate is hard – there is no doubt about it. The drop-out rate is higher than for any other activity I know. In the end I can only speak for myself: I train because I find karate a challenge. It asks questions of the body and the mind. To me karate is not a sport, although it does have a competition element. Rather, it is a living martial art – a system of training that hardens the body and strengthens the mind.

Why you train will change depending on what stage you are at in your life. But remember: karate isn't any more for the young than it is for the old. Age and gender are not deciding factors in karate development; strength of character is. Probably my finest student (who later became my wife) didn't take up karate until she was in her late twenties; my eldest daughter, on the other hand, took it up at the age of five – I couldn't find a babysitter! Both have gained so much from their training.

If you want sport and competition, then karate can offer this. If you want to know what it feels like to break a stack of tiles, karate can offer this. These are, however, diversions. If you want to learn an art that disciplines your mind and body alike, overcoming your fears and facing up to new challenges, then training in the art of *karate-do* (the way of karate) is for you.

'Karate is for life.'

What to Expect

Because of the inherent dangers involved in training in a pastime that involves people kicking and punching, you will find that karate is a very disciplined, organized activity.

Once you enter a class, don't be surprised by the mix of grades. Most clubs are not large enough to run classes solely for beginners. Consequently you could find yourself lining up alongside black belts. This should not be a problem because a good instructor will be able to cater for you as well as for the senior students. You will probably feel nervous to start off with, but that's no bad thing. It will help to keep you on your toes.

There will be points in the class where you are resting or may be out of the action. Don't switch off at these times. Watch the class, and don't let your mind wander. You can learn an awful lot by watching and listening to the instructor, even if you aren't actually performing the techniques yourself.

Each class will start with a formal bow to the instructor *(illustrated on pages 16–17)*, followed by a general warm-up to prepare you for what comes next. Classes are roughly one to two hours in duration and usually run along the lines shown on the opposite page.

You will notice that time for a warm-down is allocated at the end of the class, during which the instructor will line up the students and give them some final stretches, to help avoid stiff muscles wreaking havoc over the following days. You should find the stretches easier at this point than they were at the beginning of the class, as you will be nice and warm by this stage. I should warn you, though, that no matter how fit you are when you start your karate training, you will be using muscles you didn't even know you had, and these will ache after class. But it's a good ache – trust me.

This format for classes isn't set in stone; methods may vary from teacher to teacher. I always think that a good karate-ka can think on their feet, so expect the unexpected.

1. BASICS

These involve the practice of punches, strikes, kicks and blocks, done individually or in combination. You will tend to do them slowly to start off with, then build up speed and power.

2. KATA

Here a student goes through a set sequence of moves – something along the lines of a gymnast's set floor display. More about *kata* later.

3. KUMITE

This is pairing-up work. Here the student, depending upon grade and ability, will work together with a partner to hone their fighting skills.

4. WARM-DOWN

Stretching out at the end of a session will help prevent muscles from stiffening up afterwards.

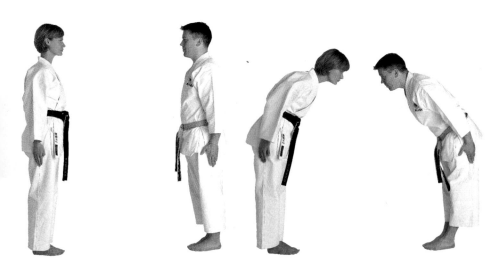

5. BOW

After bowing to their partners, the class reassembles and makes a formal bow to the instructor *(see pages 16–17)*, who then ends the class.

Finding a Dojo

When you look for a dojo to train at, you will find many to choose from. Nowadays, not least as a result of kung fu movies and the boom in martial-arts-related video rentals, clubs have sprung up all over the place. The only problem with this is that there is no regulation of such clubs. In reality, anyone can hire a hall and call themselves a master, and the public are unlikely to be any the wiser. As a general rule, avoid flashy instructors who make outlandish claims, but there are also a number of other things you can do.

WHAT TO LOOK FOR

When trying to find a dojo look around, and investigate as many clubs as possible. Always sit and watch a class first; if the instructor won't allow you to do this, ask yourself why. Look at the way the class is run. Is it organized? Does the class seem well disciplined? Ask questions of both the students and the instructor. How often should you train? What is the grading system? Is the club affiliated to a national governing body? What are the fees? Are you insured? A club secretary will be more than willing to answer these questions.

To my mind the most important thing to find is a good teacher. They come in all shapes and sizes, but when you find one stick with them. I have trained with some of the true greats of Shotokan karate and have found that they all have one thing in common: the ability to inspire. *Sensei* means 'teacher', but not just in the physical movements of karate. The Sensei should also lead by example in their manner, their spirit, and in the way they conduct themself. Karate is all about training the body in unison with the mind. Find, then, a teacher who offers all this – they do exist. Don't allow yourself to become blinkered; a true karate master doesn't have to be Japanese, just as a great chef needn't be French.

STICK WITH IT

Upon joining a dojo you will find that nearly everything you are taught feels totally alien to you. Don't let this put you off – almost every person who dons a karate *gi* (suit) feels like a fish out of water for some time. To begin with, much of what you are taught feels far removed from reality, but these early stages are the building blocks, so don't neglect them. Take time to study them properly; only through hard training and constant repetition will you have any chance of mastering the basics.

Young karate-ka being put through their paces in a traditional karate dojo. Note the use of the senior students – facing the class to demonstrate the techniques. Here we see the class practising reverse punch, Gyaku Zuki.

14

It is a common mistake with new students to want to run before they can walk. This is OK – enthusiasm is a good thing. However, don't bite off more than you can chew. Many beginners take up more than one style, flitting around between clubs. This can only harm your progress. Don't become a jack of all trades, master of none; focus on your karate, develop it, refine it, and in time, if you still have the urge to look outside your karate, choose something that will complement it. The Japanese have a saying: 'He who hunts two rabbits rarely eats rabbit pie.' Sensible advice indeed.

As a white belt, you are – in karate terms – the lowest of the low. In Japan it was common for

new students to wash the seniors' gi, polish the dojo floor and so on. These tasks should not be looked upon as menial but rather as a step on the road to learning humility. Having said this, these practices are not really relevant today – Westerners don't tend to go in for this kind of thing! But you will find that respect to your seniors and correct etiquette in the dojo are vital in your development, and we will come to this next.

Each dojo has rules, and these will be explained to you. Don't start off with the attitude that these are only for when you are wearing your gi: always conduct yourself in a calm, mature way. Training in the dojo is preparation for the real world.

Dojo Etiquette

Joining a karate class is easy – sticking with it is the hard part. It is a good idea to have some pointers as to the dos and don'ts of the dojo. Let's start at the beginning. You haven't yet invested in a karate suit, so what should you wear? I would suggest sweatpants and a sweatshirt. Don't go for figure-hugging Lycra or skimpy clothing. You will be stretching, kicking and doing all sorts of strange movements, so comfortable is best until you get your gi.

What about you? Well, first make sure you are clean and tidy – nails trimmed, hair pulled back if you wear it long. No jewellery. If you have a wedding ring, tape it up before each class if you don't want to take it off. As for clothing, whether it is a gi or not, keep it clean and well maintained at all times. Karate is all about self-discipline, so if you can't do these simple things you're in trouble.

You are now in the class. It's a good idea to speak to the instructor and let him know it's your first time. He will probably already have guessed this by the lost look on your face. The instructor will tell you where to stand when the class lines up, and will probably give you a few words of advice. Don't call him by his name – it's always 'Sensei' in the dojo.

Now a few tips. Always bow when you enter or leave the dojo (the formal bow is shown below), and always bow when you face a partner for pairing-up work. Never raise your voice in the dojo. If you have questions, ask them at the end of the class. Listen closely and copy what's going on. As I said earlier, most clubs don't have beginners classes so you will find yourself training with all grades of student. Don't be put off by this – it has its good points. If by some chance you are paired up with a senior grade, don't be frightened that you'll get hurt. As a rule they have better control than the junior grades, so are less likely to injure you – not unless you ask for it, anyway!

❶

❷

❸

THINGS YOU SHOULD KNOW

- You will be expected to train at least twice a week if you wish to grade.

- If through injury or work commitments you cannot train, you should let your instructor know.

- Always show respect to your seniors. If they help you or give advice, the word *oss* should be used to show you understand.

- Never wear a belt for a grade you have not attained. If you forget your belt, borrow one from someone the same grade or more junior.

- Never leave a class without permission from the instructor.

- At the end of the day, as long as you give 100 per cent effort you can't go far wrong. You will make mistakes – it's human – but make sure you don't keep on repeating them.

THE BOW

At the beginning and end of each class the students will line up and make a formal bow to the instructor, shown in the sequence below. It should be carried out with feeling and control. Remember: you are thanking your instructor for teaching you, so respect is essential.

Sometimes when the students are kneeling – but prior to bowing – the instructor will ask the most senior student to call out the dojo code, which is then repeated by the class. The code defines the karate-ka's code of conduct *(see page 139)*.

❶ Stand with your feet together, your hands open and your fingers pointing to the floor.
❷ Turn your feet out, bend down and at the same time slide your open hands round to the front, to rest on your knees. Hold this position until the instructor continues. Do not lose balance or kneel before the Sensei – this is disrespectful.
❸ Place your left knee on the floor, keeping your left palm resting on your leg.
❹ Bring your right knee down and sit back on your heels. Keep your back straight, hips pushed forward. Look straight ahead.
❺ Following the Sensei's lead, take your left hand and place it on the floor, pointing inwards. Don't rush.
❻ Place your right hand on the floor opposite the left, then, slowly bending from the waist, bend forward and bow. Hold the position for a moment then return upright. Don't rush to stand – wait for the instructor to lead.

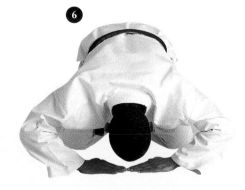

The Grading and Belt System

Probably the most common question asked by a new student is, 'How long does it take to get black belt?' The answer is always the same: it's up to you. The truth is that if you train regularly, and reach the required standard for each grade, it generally takes most people roughly three to four years. Some people take a lot longer. This isn't to say they are less able – it may just be that they decide to wait longer between grades. Getting your black belt is a great achievement, but it should never be viewed as a race.

When I started karate there were far fewer black belts around than there are today. To me, reaching that goal was just a dream, but my instructor kept my feet firmly on the ground, reminding me that each grade was a hurdle that had to be cleared. Free your mind of black belts and prepare for the next challenge ahead.

The route to black belt in the Shotokan system of karate involves ten gradings under a senior examiner. If you pass, you receive your next coloured belt – the belts tend to get darker in colour the more senior you become. Clubs have between three and four gradings a year, and the examiner will usually come from outside your club unless you are lucky enough to have joined a club with a very senior Sensei as the instructor.

A student's progress is recorded on grading cards, which the examiner refers to. This allows him to check if you have worked on the weak points previously noted. The ten levels below black belt are called *kyu* grades, and work as follows:

KYU-GRADE BELT COLOURS

10th kyu – white
9th kyu – orange
8th kyu – red
7th kyu – yellow
6th kyu – green
5th kyu – purple
4th kyu – purple with white stripe
3rd kyu – brown
2nd kyu – brown with white stripe
1st kyu – brown with two white stripes

Each examination tests your knowledge of basics, kata and kumite, and will be progressively longer and more physically demanding. You will also be tested on elements from previous gradings to make sure that you are constantly working on the basics. You must wait a minimum of three months between gradings, but the gap between 1st kyu and black belt is at least six months to allow you plenty of time to prepare for this very special examination.

THE CYCLE OF LEARNING

You will notice as you train that often a 'black' belt will have almost faded to white. This occurs when the silk in the belt wears away through years of training, revealing the white cotton beneath. As a result, very senior karate-ka can be seen to wear almost white belts. This colour change represents the evolution of the Dan grade. For, as the belt becomes white, the true karate-ka realizes that he is always a beginner with new lessons to learn.

'Humility is the mark of the warrior.'

BLACK BELT 'SHO DAN'

Once you pass black belt you are no longer a kyu grade. You now become a Sho Dan, first black belt. What does this grading involve?

Well, for the first time you will not grade at your parent club. Dan gradings are usually held at the end of special Dan-grade courses run by senior karate Sensei. These might not be local, so you will probably have to travel to them. The next change is the size of the grading. Gradings tend to involve hundreds of people, most of whom you will have never seen before. There are only a few black-belt examinations every year, so they are very well attended.

These changes, on the day of your most important grading, may seem daunting, but you must learn to take things like this in your stride. It is very easy to become comfortable with your own world – it's good for the character to be forced into a new environment. All of this is a long way off, however, so until then just worry about orange belt.

Training Regime

So you have decided to take up karate, and you have found a club with a good instructor. What now? First of all you have to be realistic as to how many times a week you train. If you are thirty-five years of age and married with four children, getting to classes might be a struggle. By the same token, if you are eighteen, single and living at home with your parents, training opportunities are more readily available. In the end it all comes down to desire: if you really want to train, you will; if you don't, excuses will pop up at an ever-increasing rate until it's easier not to train than make the effort. So, how often you train is up to you, but you must understand that, if you wish to advance, training on an irregular basis will not get you there.

REGULAR TRAINING

Karate is a very demanding art and it will ask a great deal of you. The road to success lies with regular training. If you can only train once a week due to work or other commitments, then so be it, but make sure that every time you put on your gi you give every single ounce of effort. A senior Japanese Sensei once said to me, 'Kevin, train like you will never train again.' These words fired me. It's all about giving 100 per cent, all the time.

HOW TO TRAIN

So, you train as often as you can, but how should you train? The next bit of advice was passed on to me by my instructor, Billy Higgins 6th Dan, a former world karate champion: 'Look son, never pace yourself in training – push on, push on. Your body can do more than you ever think it can.' Sensei Higgins is a true karate-ka with a will of iron, so what's good enough for him …

SPIRIT

This leads me on to my next point: listen and learn. Karate isn't just physical. Inspiration can come from a few words of encouragement from your instructor. I have trained in thousands of different classes over the years, but my strongest memories – and the ones that shaped my character – are those moments of clarity when, in the heat of kumite, you calm yourself and act in a martial way as your seniors have done. The words 'don't go down', 'keep face', 'just one more' are phrases well known to students of Sensei Enoeda. They are ground into your psyche and determine how you act. Above all, spirit is the key. Without this, all endeavour is meaningless.

MIND-SET

Much is written today about mental preparation, positive visualization and so on. It is important for a student to accept that development often comes in fits and starts. It is not uncommon to hear talk of hitting a plateau, feeling that you are treading water – not getting better, not getting worse.

We all go through stages where our training doesn't go as well as it should. My advice is: move on. If you had a bad lesson, forget it – it's behind you. Always maintain a positive attitude – just put it down to a bad day at the office. Karate is hard; it's meant to be. The quicker you set your mind to accepting this fact, the happier you will be. If you go into each class with the attitude that you are going to give it your all and really enjoy it no matter what happens, you can't go far wrong. At the end of the day you should enjoy your training, and one way to do this is to go into each class with a positive approach.

DEALING WITH INJURIES

These will occur, and all I can tell you is that, as a rule, they hurt! If you have to rest them, do. If you feel you can train, then train – it's all down to you, the student. But remember: the easy way isn't always the best way. Treat every setback as a challenge to be overcome. Whatever happens, it's character-building. As the old proverb says: 'That which does not kill us can only make us stronger.'

Main Elements

Karate training can be broken down into three main areas, all of which we have already touched on briefly earlier. Here are more details.

BASICS

Here, the student – depending upon grade and ability – practises stances, blocks, punches, strikes and kicks. As a low grade, these movements will be done separately, broken down into stages to allow the student the opportunity to study their technique and grasp the fundamental principles.

At first, movements are done slowly with great attention to detail. The final few repetitions will then be done at full speed with feeling.

KATA

Kata and its practice is a book in its own right, so what is kata? It is probably best compared to the set sequence of moves a gymnast completes when performing floor work. In the kata, the karate-ka blocks, kicks and punches imaginary opponents, and the order and direction of each move is set.

There are twenty-seven kata in the Shotokan style, each designed to develop a particular area of training, be it agility, balance, concentration, coordination, memory … the list goes on. But it's not how many kata you know that is important; it's the *way you perform them*. If you treat them purely as an athletic 'dance', you are missing the point. To many, kata are the soul of karate moves passed down to us from masters of old, so their practice should be sincere. Focus the mind as if in a trance. Don't think of where to step next or what block follows – become the kata and let it take over.

KUMITE

This is sparring, in which a student pairs off with a fellow student and starts to put into practice the basics learned earlier in the class. There are many different ways to train for *kumite*, but we'll find out more about this in Lesson Seven later on.

Theoretical Considerations

When training, it is not enough just to know the moves, getting from point A to point B without falling over. A karate-ka must understand how to make the body work to its maximum potential. Here are some things that should be taken into consideration.

KIME

Prior to every move, be it a kick, punch or block, the body should be in a relaxed state to allow the karate-ka to react in the quickest possible time. At the point of impact the whole body should tense as strongly as possible. This focus of power is called *kime*. Techniques without kime, no matter how much they may look like karate, are impostors.

ZANSHIN

As well as being relaxed prior to movement, the karate-ka should also be alert. This state of mind is called *zanshin*. You may be standing in *yoi*, ready stance, or pausing between clashes in kumite, but the mind must never switch off. Zanshin is a state of mental readiness.

SPEED

A technique without speed will have little effect. However, in your efforts to improve your karate, don't go for speed too soon. First get the technique right, then add the speed. As your training develops your technique should improve, and with it the speed of delivery. Basic moves often fail as a result of the karate-ka telegraphing his intentions by adding extra movements. Train to give nothing away. If you can do this, it will greatly enhance the speed of your attack.

Sensei Frank Brennan 6th Dan is a master of this. People marvel at the speed of his technique – however, having faced him it is not just the speed

はじめに

of his attacks that is baffling, but the incredible way he disguises his intentions by adding no superfluous movements. He combines superb technique with tremendous speed, backed up by an excellent martial spirit.

KIAI

This is the karate shout. At certain points in basic training, at focal points in the kata and upon striking an opponent in kumite, the karate-ka will use *kiai*. This shout is the link between the mind and the body. It should come from the stomach, not the throat, and should only be used at the point of greatest focus. Use of the kiai should be instinctive and – to quote Sensei Andy Sherry 7th

Dan – ferocious. It should be short, aggressive and embody your total commitment. In short, it should terrify your opponent.

BREATHING

All karate techniques involve physical exertion and, as explained earlier, the use of kime, whereby the body is tensed to concentrate power. To do this the karate-ka should breathe out sharply at the moment of focus, emptying the body of air. This state lasts for only a moment but is vital. When breathing, avoid making it too vocal – the breath should be almost silent. A simple rule to follow is to make sure the stomach is tensed to absorb a blow, and you can't go far wrong.

YOUR INSTRUCTORS

The karate-ka you will meet on the following pages – here shown in *yoi* position (ready stance) – are all students that I have trained to black-belt level. The youngest of the group – my daughter, Lauren – began training with me when she was only five, and achieved her black belt aged nine. She then went on to achieve 2nd Dan, and won the under-16 UK national championship in 1999.

Each has their own strengths and weaknesses, but the one thing they have in common is their strong attitude. They have years of karate experience between them, and have all been where you are standing now. Each one of them has achieved their personal goal through hard work and dedication. It's up to you to do the same.

KEVIN

Beginning Your Training

Y ou are now about to move on to the training section of the book. Your 'instructors' are introduced below. Together, we will take you through all the basic moves, step by step. But first, there are a couple of things you need to know.

FOOT-POSITION DIAGRAMS

Each technique includes foot-position diagrams that show you how to step. With the help of arrows, the diagrams show the movement of the feet from one stage to the next: the dotted outlines highlight the previous position of a foot, and the lighter-shaded feet indicate when a foot is 'moving through' at the midpoint of a technique. This means you should not put your full weight on it; as you improve, the foot will not stop at this point.

HINTS AND TIPS

'Points to remember' are included for each technique. Make sure you read them. From keeping your eyes on the target, to getting a high knee lift when you kick, these tips will help you to avoid the common pitfalls often encountered when performing each move. It's worth making the extra effort now so that your karate doesn't suffer later on. Practice is the key.

LAUREN

JASON

COLLETTE

鍛錬

Part Two
Training

In the pages that follow are the techniques you will come across as you start your karate training. If you have already begun training, some of these will probably be familiar. The stances, punches, strikes, blocks and kicks that are covered are the ones you will meet most in a lesson. Please don't rush when attempting to learn these movements – no matter how good you are, they take time, so give yourself that time by training regularly.

If you don't understand a point in class, refer to the relevant lesson, look up the specific technique and then work from there. A good way to learn is to practise the movement in slow motion so that every stage of the technique is correct and you are not cutting corners. Don't be embarrassed to ask senior grades to check your technique, and if the instructor pulls you up on things don't get disheartened. They are doing you a great service, as they are correcting faults early on so they do not impede your progress later.

When it comes to pairing-up work, seek as many different partners as possible. Always show respect to the senior grades and remember to exercise good control. Remember: it is a martial art, so if you take the odd knock laugh it off. We've all been there – trust me.

第一課・準備

Warming Up

When you first start training, one thing that you will notice straight away is the time taken by the instructor to give the class a thorough warm-up. The movements involved in karate practice can be very demanding, so all muscle groups should be sufficiently warmed and ready to work to their maximum.

As a rule the warm-up will start at the head and neck, and work its way down through the body. Don't neglect any area. When stretching, start slowly and gently increase the stretch. If at any time you feel pain or more than slight discomfort, release the stretch and relax. Before every class, always inform your instructor of any injuries you are carrying. Some sample stretches are included on the following pages.

At the end of the lesson the instructor will bring the class back together and go through a warm-down. You should be nice and warm by this point, so this is a perfect opportunity to stretch out. A bit of effort now, and you will miss out on a lot of aches and pains over the next few days.

CONDITIONING AND STRENGTH

Over the years, I have met instructors who see no place in training for conditioning work, stating that karate alone is enough. That's one opinion; I don't agree. To my mind, if it's good enough for boxers it's good enough for me.

If you have taken up karate for self-defence, as most people often do in the first instance (it blooms into something else later), I would suggest that the best way to deal with the stress, physical demands and overall punishment of fighting is to condition the body at every opportunity. If you take your karate seriously you will supplement your evenings at the dojo with other forms of exercise. I suggest the following:

• **Running** It doesn't have to be far – it all depends on your current level of fitness. You decide what's a good level to start at, then stick with it. Try to get some hills into your route, and do some sprints. Kumite fighting is very hard work and the stronger your heart and lungs, the better.

• **Strength Training** This doesn't mean you have to wear an extra small T-shirt and a weight-training belt! If you have access to a gym, work on light weights and lots of repetitions, developing explosive movement. You don't have to become a muscle-bound monster! If you don't like the gym you can do it all at home, with sit-ups, push-ups, squat thrusts and other similar exercises (*see page 32*). Set up a circuit involving these exercises lasting approximately twenty minutes and do it three times a week, increasing repetitions as you get stronger. You will quickly see and feel the difference. Remember:

- *The fitter you are, the quicker you recover after exercise.*
- *When you are tired your reaction time decreases.*
- *When we are tired we make mistakes.*

Every time you wear your gi, give 100 per cent.

MENTAL PREPARATION

If you are the type of person who might consider turning up at the dojo with a wet gi from two days before still stuffed into your training bag, you aren't really thinking about your training properly!

Karate training starts and ends with your attitude. Prior to training you should be checking you have everything you will need at the class: gi, belt, gumshield (women also have the option to wear breast guards for greater protection). While doing this you will begin to prepare mentally for what is ahead. Mental preparation is now accepted as vital in how a person will perform in any given scenario.

To this end, think about what you want to achieve from the class, which areas you wish to work on. Plan ahead the tactics you will use for dealing with different situations. If we think about things before they happen, they are less likely to catch us out when the time comes. Treat training as a challenge.

'Train hard, fight easy'

Warm-up Exercises

Here is a selection of some of the stretches you will be shown and expected to do prior to each class. There are many more, and each instructor will have their own favourites that they turn to. As a beginner, just getting through the warm-up can be a bit of an ordeal to start off with – turning the wrong way, losing your balance or perhaps not having a clue what the instructor means. Don't worry – we have all been there. In no time at all, everything will come together, and you will feel completely at home lining up to face the instructor for your warm-up.

STRETCHING TIPS

- Don't stretch too hard too soon.

- Try to get the body warm before attempting the stretches – a short run or a bit of skipping will do the trick.

- Always stretch at the end of a class. This will help prevent the legs and hips stiffening up in the following days.

- Make sure you stretch both sides of the body equally – don't just concentrate on one side.

- If you suffer any sudden sharp pain, stop immediately; stretching should not feel like this – trust me.

Body stretches

SIDE BEND

This stretch loosens the muscles down the side of the body. Take the left hand and place it on your hip, then stretch your right arm above your head and lean over. Keep your knees bent and your back straight. Repeat on both sides. Don't reach too far to start with: as you get warmer, reach further.

FRONT BEND

Here we stretch the main muscle groups in the backs of the legs, and you will feel the stretch in your shoulders too. Start by placing your feet apart at a comfortable distance. Keep your knees straight and slowly bend forward, placing your hands on the floor. If you aren't supple enough to reach the floor, don't worry – just go as far as you can without too much discomfort. You will feel the stretch down the back of the legs. Hold the position for a few seconds, then slowly release and come up.

TOUCHING TOES

Keeping your feet together and your legs straight, bend forward from the waist and slowly touch your toes. This one really stretches the muscles down the back of the legs. If you find it a bit hard, bend the knees slightly. If, on the other hand, you are feeling quite loosened up, try placing the backs of your hands on the floor. As with all stretches, don't bounce, as this doesn't assist the stretch and could lead to injury.

BACK STRETCH

This one does what it says! Stand with your feet apart and your hands over your head (you might find it helpful to hold your right wrist with your left hand, or vice versa). Then lean back slowly to loosen your back. Don't go too far or you may lose your balance. Make sure you keep the neck relaxed so you don't strain it.

Leg stretches

FRONT SPLITS

This stretch is a big one. You don't have to be able to do full splits to have good karate, but if you do spend time on this stretch improving your flexibility you will reap the rewards. The golden rule is: stretch often, but don't go mad. Make sure you are warm and then slowly start to drop down. This one really kills the hips, so take it easy – you will feel it tomorrow. I have heard lots of tips on making good splits, but also some really bad ones. One I like is stretching in your socks, reducing the friction and so making it harder to resist gravity. A bad one involves standing on two chairs and having other people pull them slowly apart; all I can say is reserve a place in the emergency room before you start!

THIGH STRETCH

This stretch is used to loosen the hips and stretch the muscles in the inner thigh. Don't press on the knees and don't bounce them, either. Press the soles of the feet together and then slowly let your knees fall towards the floor. If other people offer to press your knees down, don't let them! This will almost always cause injury.

STRAIGHT-LEG STRETCH

Beginners often struggle with this one as it requires some balance. Again we are stretching the muscles in the back of the leg, and at the same time stretching the muscles around the groin. To start, bend the right knee and straighten the left leg. Once in position, stretch the left leg out to increase the stretch. If you then want to increase the stretch even further, take your chest down towards your knee. Do this slowly and don't bounce. You will definitely feel this one stretching down the back of the leg.

SIDE SPLITS

Once again, this stretch is designed for hip flexibility and is a great overall stretch. Slowly drop down with one leg out in front and one stretched out behind. Remember: don't push too hard – let gravity take over. Once you feel able, try making it more difficult for yourself. Begin by making side splits and then, turning the right foot out, rotate the chest and hips and stretch to the side. This then can be repeated on the other leg.

FLOOR SPLITS

Sit on the floor and then push your legs apart as if to make the splits. Keep your legs straight and don't bend the knees. When you have found a position that you feel comfortable with, take the chest down to the centre and try to place it on the floor, then repeat on the right leg, then the left.

Don't worry if you can't get all the way down – most people can't – but work at it and you will be surprised how much this stretch increases your flexibility. To help with this stretch, you can take hold of your ankles and pull yourself gently forward.

Balance stretches

KNEE LIFT

Lift the knee, then take hold of the shin and pull your leg in towards your body as far as you can. This will help your knee lift when you kick, and at the same time stretch the leg muscles. Another good one for balance, this one. Repeat on both legs.

OUTSIDE-LEG STRETCH

A bit of a dancer's stretch this one, but great for stretching the limbs and loosening the hips. It also helps develop balance. This is not an easy stretch, so if you are struggling with it, you can miss this stretch out and move on to another one.

Strength training

SQUAT THRUSTS

Make the push-up position, legs outstretched, back straight. Then pull your legs in so that the knees touch your elbows. Don't lift up, and keep your hips down. Now thrust the legs out to their initial point, and repeat several times. This exercise is excellent for developing your fitness.

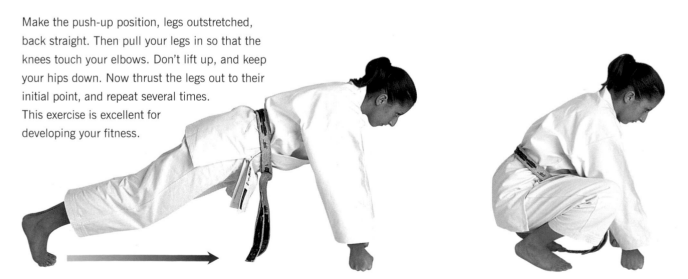

PUSH-UPS

Everyone has done push-ups of some variety. They are good for strengthening the muscles in the chest and the arms. They are often part of the warm-down at the end of a class, as they are a great way of making tired people exhausted ones! The press-up demonstrated is

designed to help your punching. Make the push-up on your fists, with the punching knuckles taking the weight. (This is not recommended for young children whose muscles and bones are still growing, as it may damage them.) Keep your elbows pressed to your side so that every time you push yourself up you feel as though you are punching out. Remember to keep your back straight and to take your chest down to the floor. Don't feel that you have to do them on your fists – open hand is fine as well. It's up to you. I prefer it, as it helps to strengthen the wrist and fist.

DON'T GIVE UP

At the end of the class the instructor often uses push-ups, sit-ups and so on to help strengthen the students. It is very easy just to go through the motions at this point. You will probably be tired and thinking of getting out of the dojo. Fight this negative attitude: even now, at the very end of the class, give everything you have. Treat it as a test of your mental strength. Don't give up – tell yourself 'just one more'. All around you people will be tired. Don't be the first to give in. As you get fitter, aim to last until the end. Treat all training as a game to harden the mind and strengthen your resolve. As with all your training, there will be good days as well as bad ones. Just remember: stick it out.

33

第二課・立

Stances • Dachi

The punches, strikes, kicks and blocks that you will read about in this book are all delivered in one of the three main Shotokan stances:

- Zenkutsu Dachi – front stance
- Kiba Dachi – horse, or straddle-leg, stance
- Kokutsu Dachi – back stance

Beginners tend to find the idea of stances a hard one to grasp, especially since in Shotokan karate the stances tend to be deeper than those of other karate styles, such as Wado Ryu. Deep stances are demanding on the leg muscles, and tire the legs of new students very quickly. As a result, when teaching it is common to see students coming up out of their stances to rest the legs. Don't do this. Stances have a number of roles, one of which is a conditioning exercise for both the mind and body. During training there will be rest periods and this is the time to recover. Fight the urge to make a higher stance. Remember: everyone else in the class is in the same boat.

Stance training is vital in your development. If you cannot control the legs and hips, how will you ever be able to deliver a technique properly? Your stance is your foundation, so make sure it's a strong one.

BASIC PRINCIPLES

Never make exaggerated stances, no matter how long-limbed or supple you are. They have no value and will not help your development in any way. When moving between stances, always keep the front knee bent and travel on the same level. When you step, imagine you are in a room with a low ceiling that is just above your head; you should feel the ceiling brushing against you, not banging off your head as you travel back and forth.

A common mistake when stepping from one stance to the next is the addition of extra movements. This is bad form, and to be avoided. Watch out for leaning forward at the start of the step, turning the front foot out as you move or, worse still, pulling the front foot back as you start to push off through the back leg. Errors such as these telegraph your intentions to your opponent.

Finally, it is very easy to feel 'strong' in the upper body, and you often see karate that is top-heavy. Avoid this by placing equal emphasis on the upper and lower body. At the completion of every technique, tense all the leg muscles so that the whole body performs the movement. As a student, you will be taught to step into a stance. This will help you to achieve a really strong stance as a result.

Front stance is the first stance taught to a karate student and the most commonly used stance in karate training. When making front stance, it is important that the stance isn't too long or too wide. Too long will inhibit movement; too wide, and you will find yourself off balance. At first you will find learning stances hard work, as the positions will seem quite unnatural. They are also very demanding on the leg muscles, but don't give up and make high, weak stances – this will hinder your progress later on. Strong stances make for strong karate.

1 Stand with your left leg forward, and your knee bent over your big toe. Your back leg should be straight, and your chest and hips square on. Keep your hands out of the way and think about staying level and balanced.

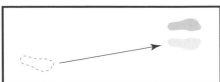

2 Bring the rear leg up to meet the front one, keeping the knees and ankles well flexed. Don't lean to assist movement. You are now at the midpoint. Push forward with the right leg, and keep your hips and chest square on .

POINTS TO REMEMBER

• Always keep your back straight – never lean.

• When moving, keep at the same level. Don't move up and down.

• As you start to step, push off hard through the rear leg, like a sprinter out of the blocks. At the midpoint, as your feet meet, use the supporting leg to drive you on.

FRONT VIEW

The legs should be hip-width apart. Check that the upper body isn't leaning to the left or right. You will often hear Japanese Sensei shouting 'push stomach', meaning 'keep your body straight, don't lean'. To check if your stance is deep enough, look down at your front leg: if you can see your big toe, you are too high, so bend a little more until your toe is hidden by your knee.

3 As your right foot lands, strongly lock the supporting leg, while at the same time making sure your front knee is well bent and aligned over your toes. Check your hips and chest are square on. To step again, repeat the sequence on the opposite side.

後屈立

ack stance is one of the hardest movements to master in karate, and because of this it is often neglected. The difficulty arises from the fact that the movement is alien to most people. Back stance demands that the karate-ka must work with his heels in line, making balance awkward. As well as having 70 per cent of the weight on the rear leg and 30 per cent on the front leg, the knees must be pushed out at right angles to one another and the hips must be kept level. Back stance is found in nearly all kata, so it is vital to come to terms with it at an early stage in your karate training or your kata will suffer.

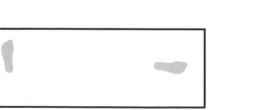

1 Stand with your right leg forward and your feet at right angles to one another. Your heels should be in line. Bend both knees, but keep 70% of your weight on the back leg. Open your chest, and keep your face in line with your front knee.

FRONT VIEW

1a The heels should be in line and the knees pushed out, and the chest and hips should be open. Your chin should be in line with your front knee. This stance is very demanding on the ankles and knees, so don't rush the movement – make it smooth.

POINTS TO REMEMBER

• Don't make the stance too long or the rear knee will dip inwards. Remember to push out the knees.

• Don't stamp when stepping.

• There is a tendency to lean backwards in this stance, so make sure you keep both hips level.

• Start slowly and work on smooth movement on a level plane.

2 Bring the rear leg up to meet the front one, keeping the knees and ankles well flexed. Don't lift up as you move. You are now at the midpoint. Step forward with the left leg, keeping the sole of the foot close to the floor. Don't raise the heel of the supporting leg as you start to move – this will cause loss of power.

3 Slide your left foot into place, and as you do so twist your hips and turn the supporting foot out, pivoting on your heel. The heels should now be in line and the knees pushed up and out at right angles to each other, with the weight distribution 70/30 from rear leg to front one.

Kiba Dachi • Horse Stance

Horse, or straddle-leg, stance is similar to back stance in that the heels are in line, only here both feet are turned in and the knees are pushed out. This aids balance. It is particularly demanding on the legs and knee joints, but is a very powerful stance, and you should feel rooted to the spot when it is executed correctly. Always keep your back straight and don't fall into the trap of leaning back. At first you will find it very tiring on the leg muscles, but (as with all karate training) don't give in and come up out of the stance – stick with it and reap the rewards.

1 Stand with your left leg forward, your heels in line, and your feet slightly inverted. Grip the floor with your toes. Centre your weight and bend your knees, pushing them outwards, creating tension in the legs.

2 Bring the rear leg up to meet the front one, but, unlike in front and back stance, don't freeze at the midpoint – carry on and cross the legs over. Keep the knees well bent and your back straight.

第二課・立

This stance has three kata (formal exercises) built around it, and so is of great importance in the karate grading syllabus. Do not neglect it.

POINTS TO REMEMBER

• Stretch well before using this stance, as it makes great demands on the muscles and joints.

• You should always feel that the weight is evenly proportioned between both legs.

• Avoid moving up and down when delivering the technique – keep level.

SIDE VIEW

Note the feet are in line, with the toes turned in, gripping the floor. The knees are bent and pushed out, creating tension in the legs. Keep your back straight, and always face the direction of travel. When moving, don't lift upwards – keep your knees bent, and glide through.

3 Now step out with the left leg into horse stance. As you land, turn your feet in and push your knees out. Remain at the same level throughout the movement.

第三課・突

Punching • Zuki

The first step in learning to punch is making a correct karate fist *(see below)*. Making the fist is straightforward enough; conditioning it into a powerful weapon is another matter. This can only be done through years of rigorous training. In the past, karate-ka would strike straw pads called *makiwara* (more about these on page 127). These rough striking posts were used as a conditioning tool, and were the place where karate-ka honed their kime. Nowadays, however, the makiwara is rarely seen in a dojo.

As a rule, in basic training karate punches travel in a straight line from the hip. The fist, which is inverted at the starting point, rotates only upon impacting with the target. The karate-ka should aim to hit the target with the two most prominent knuckles of the fist.

As a student becomes more advanced, usually around brown-belt level, they will instinctively start to hold the hands in a more natural way, usually known as freestyle (*kamae*). At this point they will start to snap the punch back as in kumite practice, as opposed to delivering the punch and leaving the arm in position until the next movement.

The reason behind the delay in allowing a student to move on to snap punch is to allow sufficient time for the development of a straight, strong karate punch that can be controlled. Only when they can demonstrate that they can do this will they be allowed to advance to the next stage. However, this is not the end of the story. If you attend any class – even those containing the most senior grades – you will see them practising basic punching movements. Always return to your basics.

In the pages that follow are some of the karate punches you will need to know to begin your study of karate. There are many more, and in time you will be shown them, too. During class you will repeat thousands of punches – never let them become stale. Always think about what you are doing; try to make them faster, stronger; never be happy with your technique.

MAKING A FIST

1 Stretch the hand out flat, with the palm facing downwards.

2 Open the thumb and bend the ends of the fingers over, keeping them tightly together.

3 Now roll the fingers so that they are tightly 'shut' into the palm of the hand.

4 Wrap the thumb under the gripped fingers to seal the fist. Keep the wrist straight and the punching knuckles prominent.

直突

Choku Zuki is the classic karate punch, delivered in a straight line to the target, the fist travelling inverted from the hip but rotating at the point of impact. Correct timing of the technique is essential, so start slowly but with feeling. Don't just think of the punching arm – remember to develop the returning arm too, so that even standing still you are developing your whole body. It is important to remember when practising karate that no movement should ever be done in a casual manner. Even when working slowly on a technique such as the punch, do it with the correct mental attitude and attention to detail. Working in slow motion can be used to great advantage as a type of resistance training.

1 Stand with your feet apart (Hachiji Dachi position). Hold your left arm out in front of you in line with your solar plexus, and your right fist, inverted, just above the hip bone. You should be relaxed but alert.

SIDE VIEW

1a Note that the shoulders are level, the back is straight and the chin is down. Make sure you don't drop your chin too far when executing your technique – eye contact is vital, so never look down at the floor. This is a common mistake with beginners, and one that is hard to get out of once learned.

POINTS TO REMEMBER

- Keep the body relaxed prior to executing the punch.

- Don't tense or raise your shoulders in an attempt to gain power.

- You should feel your elbows rubbing against your sides as you punch – this will stop you 'hooking' your punch.

- Upon impact. tense the whole body from the calves up. Without this focus, it is not a karate punch.

- Start slowly, but once it has started to come together work on speed. Add multiple punches and develop exact kime – here, you focus for a split second each time you impact a target.

2 Keeping your shoulders down, slowly drive your right fist out towards the target. At the same time, begin to withdraw the extended arm. At this midpoint the elbows should be pressed against your sides.

3 Drive the punching arm out while at the same time withdrawing the reaction arm. Don't let your shoulders rise up. It is vital you don't twist either fist yet – leave that to the very last moment, when you complete the punch with kime.

4 Now fully extend the punching arm, rotating the fist at the very last moment. Simultaneously, the reaction arm should be returning to your side, twisting strongly back into an inverted position. Remember – maximum tension at the moment of striking.

45

Oi Zuki • Stepping Punch

Oi Zuki, or stepping punch, is one of the first techniques students generally learn. It combines the delivery of the basic karate twisting punch with the use of the front stance Zenkutsu Dachi *(see page 36)*. It is one of the most direct and powerful techniques in karate, as it involves a strong stepping action combined with the karate-ka using his full body weight. No momentum or balance is lost in spinning, making it a commonly used attack.

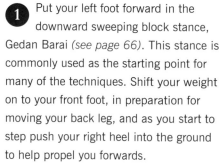

1 Put your left foot forward in the downward sweeping block stance, Gedan Barai *(see page 66)*. This stance is commonly used as the starting point for many of the techniques. Shift your weight on to your front foot, in preparation for moving your back leg, and as you start to step push your right heel into the ground to help propel you forwards.

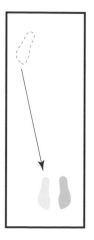

2 Pull the rear leg up alongside the front leg, keeping level as you move. The hips should now be square on. Don't straighten your legs – keep both knees and ankles well flexed, so they can act like springs to propel you forwards as you punch. Hold your right elbow tight against your side, which will help to keep the punch straight. Hold your left arm forwards horizontally.

POINTS TO REMEMBER

• Keep your back straight and eyes up, looking straight at the target. Never over-reach.

• If you step too slowly your opponent will have time to evade the punch, so always keep it quick.

STRIKE AREA

Note that the thumb is held well back out of the way to avoid injury. Use it to help bind your fist together. The knuckles of the index and middle fingers (known as *seiken*) are used to strike the target.

SIDE VIEW

Twist the fist through 180 degrees at the very last second to give maximum kime (focus) to the point of impact. On completion of the punch, the whole body should be square on, driving the full body into the attack. Note how the back leg remains straight when the punch is executed.

3 Keeping the hips and shoulders square, step forward with your right leg into front stance. At the last moment drive the punching arm (right) out to the target. Simultaneously pull the reaction arm (left) back strongly. Just before you are about to strike the target, rotate the punching fist. Remember to tense the fist and wrist and to strike with the two prominent knuckles *(see Strike Area above)*. Only tense your body at the point of impact, so you don't telegraph your intentions.

逆突

Gyaku Zuki, or reverse punch, is one of karate's most popular techniques. It is regularly used in kumite (sparring), as it is easily deployed as a counter-attack. It is essential when delivering this punch that the hips and chest are only employed at the very last moment prior to impact with the target, to maximize power.

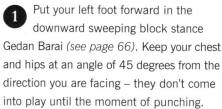

1 Put your left foot forward in the downward sweeping block stance Gedan Barai (see page 66). Keep your chest and hips at an angle of 45 degrees from the direction you are facing – they don't come into play until the moment of punching.

2 Without moving the chest and hips, start to make right hand reverse punch by moving your punching arm forward and pulling your reaction arm back. Keep your elbows close to your sides to avoid hooking the punch.

第三課・突

3 Now fully extend the punching arm, and push your hips and chest into the technique to maximize power. At the same time, pull the reaction arm back to your side. Tense the back leg strongly to absorb the impact of the blow when it lands. Make sure you are punching to the centre, in front of your solar plexus. Note the width of the stance: too wide, and you won't be able to use your hips correctly when you punch; too narrow, and the rotation of the hips and chest will take you off balance.

SIDE VIEW

Don't just concentrate on rotating the right hip and side of your chest as you punch. If, at the same time, you pull your left hip and side of chest back along with the recovery of the reaction arm, this will greatly speed up the punch as well as adding further power. This pushing and pulling of the body is vital in developing true karate. Note that the front knee is now fully committed.

POINTS TO REMEMBER

• The punch must land at the same time as the hip twist – easier said than done, as the hand has much further to travel. Timing is everything with this technique.

• 'Keep face.' Anyone who has trained regularly with the Japanese will have heard this expression. Basically, don't take your eyes off your opponent. Even though your body is twisting, don't let your head turn away with it.

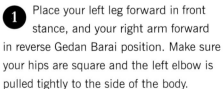

Kizami Zuki, or leading hand punch, is delivered with the front hand (the hand on the same side as the forward leg in front stance). Normally executed to the face, this punch can best be described as a stopping technique, in that as your opponent starts to attack you move in and take the initiative, punching to the face before the attacker has time to deliver his own attack.

1 Place your left leg forward in front stance, and your right arm forward in reverse Gedan Barai position. Make sure your hips are square and the left elbow is pulled tightly to the side of the body.

2 Keeping your left elbow pressed tightly against your side, start to punch. Keep the punching fist inverted and don't start to move the chest and hips yet. As with reverse punch, the rotation happens at the last moment.

3 The split second before impact, rotate your hips and chest to 45 degrees and twist the punching fist. This rotation increases your reach to the target. Also, to add power, push your left knee towards the opponent. Don't forget to draw the reaction arm back to your side, inverting the fist, and tense the body strongly on impact. The two punching knuckles should be aligned directly in front of your chin.

SIDE VIEW

Note that the punching fist is in line with the chin. When attacking to the head in basic training, always aim for your own head height.

POINTS TO REMEMBER

• Don't allow your front elbow to stick out as you punch; this will take the punch off line, as well as damaging the elbow joint.

• On impact, make sure the muscles around the shoulders and sides are tensed strongly to absorb the blow.

第四課・打

Striking • Uchi

Striking encompasses the use of elbow as well as hand attacks – both types are included in this lesson. With punching, the elbow is locked and the fist is thrust to the target, whereas striking with the hand involves bending the elbow and then using it as a pivot. The hand 'snaps' forward and back as it hits the target, in much the same way that front kick (Mae Geri; *see page 78*) snaps back immediately after delivery.

You will see that the strike can use both the open and closed hand as a weapon, as well as the point of the elbow. The power is generated by the speed of the snapping action, as in Uraken, or back fist strike *(see page 54)*. These attacks are best used for close-in fighting, when kicks and punches are restricted. Strikes also lend themselves to use in bag work (more about this on page 126), and any serious karate-ka will not neglect their development as part of his training programme.

When used correctly, strikes can be devastating. The crucial point here is that they are designed to be aimed at extremely vulnerable areas such as the throat, eyes, temple and so on. Because of the target areas involved, it is therefore vital that they are well controlled. The use of open-hand techniques in competition karate is banned in most styles for this very reason, and elbow attacks are rarely seen. Occasionally, however, someone comes along who is able to incorporate these attacks into their kumite – Sensei Yahara of the Japan Karate Association being one. The important thing to remember is that control is the key.

STRIKING TIPS

• Remember: strikes can be extremely powerful, so great care must be taken when applying them in partner work.

• When attempting to incorporate these techniques into your armoury, start slowly and make sure that you are using them in the correct situations, when distance is close and hand and foot attacks are limited due to range.

Back fist strike has two variations. In the first it travels in a circular action to the temple; upon striking the target it returns via the same route. In the second it again takes a circular motion but this time in a downward direction, striking the bridge of the nose. The striking area is the back of the hand.

1 Stand in front stance, left leg forward, with your guard held in the freestyle (kamae) position. Your elbows should rest against your sides, and your body should be held at 45 degrees to offer less of a target.

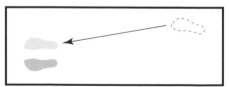

2 Step with the rear leg to the midpoint. At the same time, pull your right fist to the left side of your face in preparation for the attack. Push the reaction arm out, but keep your shoulders down and body square.

第四課・打

Don't hit with the back of the hand. Use only the conditioned area – the knuckles – when you strike.

POINTS TO REMEMBER

• Don't lose control of the striking elbow, as this controls the attack.

• Don't just rely on the snap of the strike for its effectiveness; make sure you get your hips and chest into the strike for maximum power.

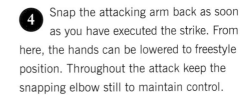

4 Snap the attacking arm back as soon as you have executed the strike. From here, the hands can be lowered to freestyle position. Throughout the attack keep the snapping elbow still to maintain control.

FRONT VIEW

The striking fist is in line with the chin. The body twist increases reach and maximizes power.

3 Extend the right arm in a snapping action and attack to the side of the jaw, keeping your elbow firmly in place. As you strike, twist your body to 45 degrees, and pull the reaction arm back to your side.

底掌打

Teisho Uchi • Palm Heel Strike

As your karate training develops, you will discover that the fists and feet are not the only weapons. Teisho Uchi, or palm heel strike, utilizes the heel area of the hand: the wrist is bent back, with the fingers and thumb tightly clenched. This method of attack is usually aimed at the jaw. Upon striking the target, the fingers can then reach out and attack the eyes. Teisho is a close-range attack and a very effective one.

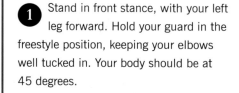

1 Stand in front stance, with your left leg forward. Hold your guard in the freestyle position, keeping your elbows well tucked in. Your body should be at 45 degrees.

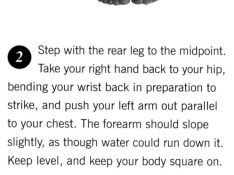

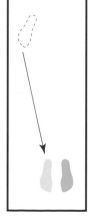

2 Step with the rear leg to the midpoint. Take your right hand back to your hip, bending your wrist back in preparation to strike, and push your left arm out parallel to your chest. The forearm should slope slightly, as though water could run down it. Keep level, and keep your body square on.

For maximum effect, drive the strike out as far as you can, locking your elbow joint in the process.

STRIKE AREA

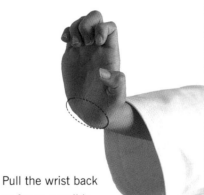

Pull the wrist back as far as possible, gripping the thumb and fingers tightly back, out of the way. Strike with the heel of the hand.

3 Now step forward with the right leg into front stance, and drive the palm heel forwards and upwards towards the opponent's jaw. Be sure to drive your hips and chest into the technique, to give greater force to the strike.

POINTS TO REMEMBER

• Start slowly. Make sure you are hitting with the right part of the hand.

• Keep your fingers well out of the way; open, they are easily broken.

Shuto Uchi, or knife hand strike, uses the outside ridge of the hand as the striking area. This area, from the base of the little finger down to the wrist, is surprisingly strong. Often when karate-ka demonstrate *tamashiwara* (breaking techniques), this is one of the strikes used. The power for this technique comes from the circular route of the attack. The knife hand is normally aimed at the throat or neck. Great care must be exercised when carrying out this technique, as the open hand can easily catch the opponent in the eyes.

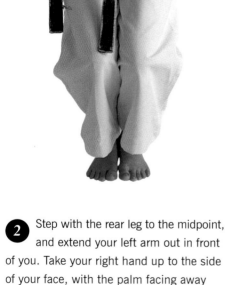

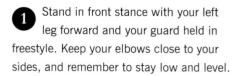

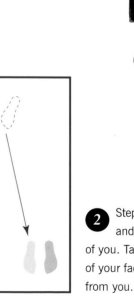

1 Stand in front stance with your left leg forward and your guard held in freestyle. Keep your elbows close to your sides, and remember to stay low and level.

2 Step with the rear leg to the midpoint, and extend your left arm out in front of you. Take your right hand up to the side of your face, with the palm facing away from you.

58

SIDE VIEW

As the hand is about to strike the target, invert the wrist sharply using a strong twisting action. Make sure to strike with the ridge of the hand and not the side of the fingers.

STRIKE AREA

Strike with the edge of the hand from the base of the little finger to the wrist. Bend the thumb back firmly to help tense the hand and make the attack stronger.

3 Step forward with the right leg and attack with the right arm to the neck. Your left arm should simultaneously return to your left hip. Make sure your hips and chest are turning in time with the attack.

POINTS TO REMEMBER

• Be sure to keep the thumb well bent, as this helps strengthen the wrist area when striking.

• Even though the knife hand attack will feel strong due to its circular route, make sure you are still getting your hips into the movement for maximum force.

59

回猿臂打

Mawashi Empi • Round House Elbow Strike

Empi, or elbow attacks, are designed for close-in fighting. These strikes are short, fast and devastating if landed without control. Because they are used at close range, it means the opponent has little or no time to see them or get out of the way. Always strive to get maximum force into the technique through fluid use of the hips and chest.

1 Stand in front stance, left leg forward, with your guard held in freestyle. Remember to keep your elbows tucked into your sides.

2 Step with the rear leg to the midpoint. Push your left arm out in front of you – this will help to push away your opponent – and bring your right fist back to your hip.

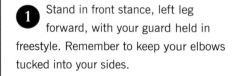

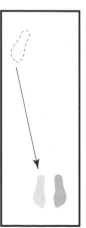

第四課・打

POINTS TO REMEMBER

• Distance is vital with this attack – make sure you get in close to your opponent.

• The point of the elbow is very hard, so be sure to exercise good control in partner work.

SIDE VIEW

The striking arm should travel in one plane when executing this attack.

STRIKE AREA

Always strike with the point of the elbow, not the forearm. Remember: this is a very strong attack, so good control is essential.

3 Rotate the hips and chest, and at the same time drive the right elbow in a circular action towards the target. Don't let the fist drop, and don't raise the elbow. As the strike lands, place the right fist squarely on the chest. The right arm should travel on one plane.

揚
猿
臂
打

Rising elbow strike is designed to attack under the jaw, knocking the head back as it lands. As with all elbow strikes, it should only be contemplated for close-in fighting. Remember: getting in really close to your opponent does have its advantages and is a vital part of realistic training for combat, but don't forget that if you are in range, so is he. The nearer you are to an opponent, the less time you have to react to attacks. Always keep this in mind. The truth is that at some point you will get hit, so be prepared.

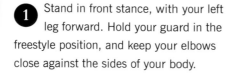

1 Stand in front stance, with your left leg forward. Hold your guard in the freestyle position, and keep your elbows close against the sides of your body.

2 Step with the rear leg to the midpoint, and push the reaction arm out in front of you to deflect your opponent. Simultaneously, pull the fist of the striking arm back to your hip.

第四課・打

3 Step with the right leg into front stance, and at the same time drive the rising elbow up to the target – in this case, underneath the attacker's jaw, pushing the head back. As before, twist the hips and chest into the attack, rotating the body to 45 degrees. When you start the rising elbow attack, try to keep your fist as close as possible to the side of your face, so that it brushes your cheek. This will keep the attack nice and tight.

STRIKE AREA

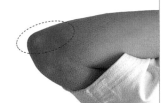

Again, strike with the point of the elbow. Try to press your forearm into the bicep to strengthen the attacking arm.

SIDE VIEW

As you complete the strike, drive the elbow as high as you can – your reach should improve with practice.

POINTS TO REMEMBER

• Keep the striking arm pressed tightly against the side of your face on impact.

• Don't allow your head to turn away as you hit.

• Try to grab hold of your opponent, to stop him escaping or leaning back to avoid the strike.

第五課・受

Blocking • Uke

In this section we will look at five blocks. They will teach you to defend against attacks to the head and body. There are a number of other blocks that you will come across as your training advances, but these five will sustain you from beginner through to black belt.

In the early stages of your training, all blocks except knife hand block will be done with a clenched fist. Later you will move on to open-hand blocks, which are more applicable to freestyle.

When blocking, always try to achieve two aims: to deflect the attack without being hit, and to put yourself in a position to make a strong counter. Never just block.

Correct timing is vital – get this wrong on a regular basis and there is a danger that friends and relatives won't recognize you! In training, always seek out a partner who will try to make his attacks land; this way, you will know if the block works.

When you first start training, it is usually the blocking section of the lesson that beginners find most painful, although not unbearable – trust me. This will soon pass, so don't go out and buy all sorts of pads to protect your arms and shins: in the short term, you will miss out on those bruises, but you will have failed to condition your arms to the effects of strong blocks as well as showing a weak attitude in the face of pain. To quote Sensei Billy Higgins, 'Pain is a great teacher.'

BLOCKING TIPS

• Get the distance right. If, in your attempts to escape an attack, you step back so far as to be unable to make an immediate counter, you have missed the point. The moment you block, counter – any delay will allow your opponent time to react. Distance is vital.

• Never reach for an attack. Always let it come to you, then deflect it at the last moment when it is committed.

Gedan Barai • Downward Sweeping Block

As you will have already seen, a large part of basic training starts from the left leg forward Gedan Barai position. This block is primarily used to defend against mid-section kicks. It is certainly one of the more powerful blocks, as it makes full use of the hips and chest.

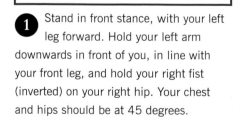

1 Stand in front stance, with your left leg forward. Hold your left arm downwards in front of you, in line with your front leg, and hold your right fist (inverted) on your right hip. Your chest and hips should be at 45 degrees.

2 Step with the right leg to the midpoint. At the same time take your right fist up to the left side of your face, keeping the elbow pressed down. The left arm should point down to the ground, the hand open, and both arms should be squeezed together. Make sure you haven't lifted up – keep your knees bent.

POINTS TO REMEMBER

• Don't swing the arm down – drive it as though you are striking.

• Make sure you don't block too high. The blocking hand should be roughly the width of a fist above the front knee.

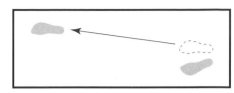

3 Now step with the right leg into front stance, and at the same time drive the right fist down to block. The left arm should be pulled back to the hip. This movement will help turn the body to 45 degrees. As you land, be sure to lock your back leg. The front knee should be well bent.

FRONT VIEW

2a Note that the knees and feet are together and the body is square on. Remember to press your elbows together and keep your shoulders down. Don't let your right elbow rise up – keep the point of the elbow in line with your solar plexus. This position should feel very compact, ready to explode into the block.

揚受

Age Uke • Rising Block

ising block, or Age Uke, is designed to deflect blows to the head. Upon completion, the blocking arm should be above the head at an angle of 45 degrees. At the same time, the body should twist to 45 degrees to assist deflection of the attack.

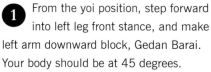

1 From the yoi position, step forward into left leg front stance, and make left arm downward block, Gedan Barai. Your body should be at 45 degrees.

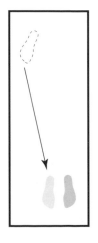

2 Step with the rear leg, and at the same time point your left arm in front of your face. At this midpoint your body should be square on to the target. Remember not to lift up when you step – keep your knees bent and your shoulders relaxed.

POINTS TO REMEMBER

• Even though you use your arms to block, make sure your feet get you out of danger. Always step quickly.

• When using the basic blocks, never lean away to avoid the attack. Escaping the attack in this way stops you from testing the effectiveness of the block.

• Never 'just block'; always train to counter-attack.

SIDE VIEW

Make sure your hips and chest are now at 45 degrees, allowing you to counter-attack. It's a common mistake with junior grades to look up as the block is executed. Don't. Look directly ahead, and maintain eye contact with your opponent.

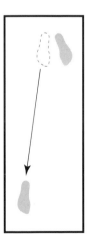

3 Now step with the right leg and keep the right fist pinned to the hip until the last possible moment. Then, as the foot lands, drive the right fist up from the hip, travelling in front of the face, pulling your left fist back to your side at the same time. The blocking arm should twist over in the same way that a punch does at the point of impact. This twist helps deflect the attack. Both hands should twist together at the very last moment.

Ude Uke • Outside Block

Of the two mid-section blocks, this one is the strongest. It is also the block most beginners struggle with. Start slowly and break it down into separate parts, but still attempt to make each movement as fluid as possible. This block really is bone on bone, and it will hurt to start off with, but don't be put off.

1 From the yoi stance, step forward into front stance with your left leg, Gedan Barai position. Your body should be at 45 degrees.

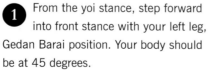

2 Step with the rear leg and, as you start to move, point your left arm out in front of your chest and pull the right arm up and back so that your right fist is behind your head, palm side outwards. Your body should now be square on, knees bent, keeping low and level.

70

3 Now step with the right leg. As with rising block, keep the blocking arm back until the last moment. As the right foot lands, drive the right forearm down and across your mid-section, covering the area in front of your chest. Twist the blocking arm at the end of the technique. This block can be used to deflect both kicks and punches.

SIDE VIEW

As with all other blocks, the body travels through 45 degrees, helping to drive the block forward.

POINTS TO REMEMBER

• Don't reach for the attack – let it come to you.

• Make sure you block with the area just below the wrist.

• Don't block too close to your body, as the blocking area is small, and if you miss the attack you may get hit. Remember: fast feet to evade the attack and a strong block to deflect it.

Uchi Uke • Inside Block

Inside block is the other mid-section block, and can also be used to deflect both kicks and punches. It is easier to learn than outside block but not as strong, and for this reason it's not used as much in partner work.

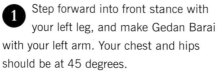

1 Step forward into front stance with your left leg, and make Gedan Barai with your left arm. Your chest and hips should be at 45 degrees.

2 Step forward with the rear leg, and at the same time extend the left arm in front of your chest, taking your right arm (with the blocking fist) across your body under the left. The fist should sit just above the hip. Your body should be square on and your knees bent, ready to move.

POINTS TO REMEMBER

• When you make the block, control the elbow – don't let it 'wobble', as this will weaken the movement.

• Don't block too close to your body, or you may get hit.

• Don't let the block ride up – check that the blocking fist is level with your shoulders.

SIDE VIEW

The head is up, and eye contact is good. Make sure you don't allow the blocking elbow to get too close to the body, as this will increase the chances of being hit.

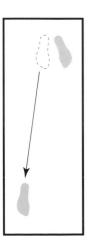

3 Now step with the right leg – try to keep the body square on until the last moment. As the right foot lands, block across your chest from the inside out, twisting the hips and chest to 45 degrees to increase power and to reduce the target area you are offering your opponent. The blocking fist should finish in line with your front knee.

手刀受

Knife hand block is the first open-hand technique a student will come across. The fact that it is used in conjunction with back stance – all other techniques coming from front stance – makes it doubly difficult. The outer ridge of the hand is used to make the block, and this causes two potential problems: first, it is such a small part of the hand that it is easy to miss the target; and second, beginners often injure themselves, blocking with the fingers instead.

1a

2a

1 Stand in back stance with your left leg forward – check your heels are in line and your back is straight. Your right hand should be inverted, placed covering your solar plexus, and your left arm should be out in front of you with the elbow bent and hand open, palm facing downwards.

2 Step with your right leg to the midpoint and, as you start to step, point your left hand out in front of your chest. At the same time, take your right hand to the left side of your face, with the palm of the hand facing your cheek. You are now square on, knees bent.

74

POINTS TO REMEMBER

• Throughout the block, keep the fingers rigid and the thumbs well bent.

• At the end of the movement, check that your front foot, knee, blocking elbow and chin are in line.

• Make sure you leave the twist in the hands until the very last moment. Don't let your hands just swing to the target.

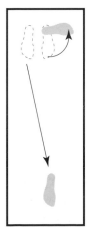

SIDE VIEW

The feet are at right angles to each other, and the weight is predominantly on the rear leg. The reaction arm should remain open and twist into place on the solar plexus, and the hand should be level with the elbow of the blocking arm. Don't straighten the blocking arm too much, as this will reduce the power of the block – the arm should form a triangle.

3 Keeping the hands still, step with the right foot into back stance. Don't let all your weight fall forward and then rock back into the stance as an afterthought – keep the weight on the supporting leg. At the last moment, pivot on the left heel at right angles; coincide this twist with the blocking action of the hands. As you pull the left hand back, drive your right hand down and across from your face, stopping the block in line with the knee. Feel the hands cutting through the air as they twist.

第六課・踢

Kicking • Geri

It cannot be denied that mastery of kicking greatly increases the threat the karate-ka poses to an opponent. The legs are longer than the arms, therefore increasing the range at which you can strike an opponent. But they are also heavier than the arms, too, and this weight makes them considerably harder to block.

Don't fall into the trap of thinking that unless you are extremely supple (able to do full side splits and the like!) you can't kick to a high standard. Effective kicking isn't about height of kick; after all, the head is only one of many targets available to you. Some styles of karate have no head kicks at all in their syllabus, realizing that some of the most devastating kicks can be directed to the groin, knees and shins.

This said, it is true that if you are supple you will kick with greater ease, and this in turn will tend to increase the speed of the kick. The golden rule for all karate-ka is stretch, stretch, and then when you have finished, stretch some more.

Due to the demands made on balance when kicking, the muscles used in the legs and any injuries sustained in the knees and hips will be strained if you fail to warm up correctly or don't use the correct technique. Beginners as a rule find training in kicking the most demanding aspect of basic training. Don't rush your kicks. At this stage you are attempting to learn something completely alien to you. The best way forward is to work slowly, developing leg strength and balance.

Kicking tends to draw the most attention because it can be very spectacular. Don't focus on leg work to the detriment of your punching or blocking. What if you have a leg injury: is training over? Not at all – you work on other areas. Play games with your mind, think of different scenarios and how you would cope if you couldn't block, for example, or kick with your best leg. You are learning to fight; part of this must be an acceptance of pain and injury. Be adaptable at all times.

There are four kicks included in this lesson. You will find some of them very difficult, as they involve the use of spinning techniques in addition to maintaining your balance on one leg. Keep practising – you *will* improve.

KICKING TIPS

• Always work on a quick, high knee lift. If it is slow or too low, your kick will suffer.

• As a rule, kicks have a long way to travel to the target. If you telegraph your intention by tensing your face, leaning, or adding extra movements, the kick will have little chance of success.

• No matter what the type of kick, be it snap or thrust, always recover it and get your foot back to the floor as fast as possible.

• Kicking can be very tiring – if you intend to use kicks don't just throw them and hope for the best. See a target and hit it. At the very least make sure your opponent has to block.

Mae Geri • Front Kick

Front kick is the first kick a beginner is taught. It is the most direct kick, and technically the easiest to grasp. However, in kumite it is the least used of the kicks. This is probably due to the confidence required to execute it correctly. Front kick can be directed to the head, body or *gedan* – the groin area.

1 From the yoi position, step forward into left leg front stance. Hold your arms in the freestyle position. At this point, keep the upper body relaxed, especially the shoulders. Any tension here will slow the kick.

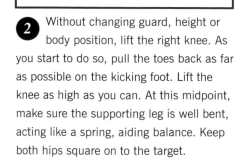

2 Without changing guard, height or body position, lift the right knee. As you start to do so, pull the toes back as far as possible on the kicking foot. Lift the knee as high as you can. At this midpoint, make sure the supporting leg is well bent, acting like a spring, aiding balance. Keep both hips square on to the target.

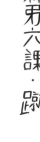

POINTS TO REMEMBER

• When starting the kick, don't telegraph the attack by adding extra movements, such as moving the arms or head prior to the kick.

• Make sure you push both hips into the kick.

• Never lean backwards to gain height – always rely on a good knee lift to give your kick greater range.

STRIKE AREA

Pull the toes back as far as you can and aim to land with the ball of the foot. Remember to point the foot into the attack, so that you don't hit with the sole of the foot.

FRONT VIEW

The kick should be straight, in line with your chin. Note the bend in the supporting knee, and that the body is square on – don't let it twist as you deliver the kick.

3 Kick out with the right leg, and at the same time push both hips forward into the attack. Strike the target with the ball of the foot. Make sure you don't lock the supporting leg. Remember that your knee is acting like a spring here, so keep it bent to absorb the impact of striking the target.

4 Upon striking the target, snap the kicking leg back to its mid-point position. Feel the calf pressed against the back of the thigh. By doing this you will be sure to have snapped the kick back correctly. A common mistake with kicking is not recovering the leg sharply once the kick has been delivered. This leaves you vulnerable to a counter-attack. Recover the kick quickly, and then you have the option of stepping forward or returning the foot to the starting point.

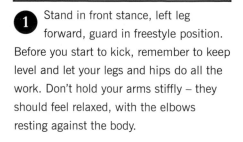

Side thrust kick makes full use of the thrusting action of the leg. The kick is almost always directed to the mid-section, and the point of contact is the side edge of the foot (*sukuto*). This kick is difficult to master as it involves being able to hold the leg out while at the same time using a strong twisting action from the supporting leg. You will find this one of the most tiring of kicks. Make sure you have stretched fully before executing it.

1 Stand in front stance, left leg forward, guard in freestyle position. Before you start to kick, remember to keep level and let your legs and hips do all the work. Don't hold your arms stiffly – they should feel relaxed, with the elbows resting against the body.

2 Lift the right knee as high as you can, while keeping the supporting leg bent. Aim to lift the knee between the gap in your arms so that you don't have to move them prior to kicking, thus telegraphing your intention. As in front kick, pull the toes back as far as you can. Relax your shoulders.

FRONT VIEW

Note that the supporting foot has twisted to allow full use of the hips. The kicking foot is slightly angled and the body is in an upright position. Eye contact is maintained with the opponent throughout – even when doing a high kick like this.

3 Drive the kick out to the target, and at the same time twist the supporting foot 180 degrees, pivoting on the heel. This twist is vital in order to kick correctly, making maximum use of the hips. Remember to keep upright and to kick with the side edge of the foot. Your guard should still be up and the hands relaxed, ready to continue.

STRIKE AREA

Strike with the side edge of the foot. The big toe should be pulled back as in front kick, but the other toes should be turned down, curling under. This helps to strengthen the foot and ankle prior to striking the target.

4 At this point, don't ruin the kick by failing to return it to its starting point. Remember that if you don't bring it back quickly, your opponent will have the opportunity to grab your leg and disable you.

POINTS TO REMEMBER

• Most people tend to swing the leg to the target or let it ride up. Avoid this by using a very high knee lift.

• This kick is greatly weakened the more you lean away from the target. Try to keep upright. Height isn't important – power and accuracy are.

• This kick demands great muscle control. If you are struggling, use a wall or chair for balance and practise holding the leg out.

Mawashi Geri • Round House Kick

Round house kick is one of the more spectacular karate techniques. It travels in an arc towards the target – unlike the previous kicks, which come straight at you. It can be used to attack either the head or body – *jodan* or *chudan*. Hip flexibility is vital for this kick to be executed correctly. When kicking to the face, train to kick with both the ball of the foot and the instep; the first being the classical interpretation, the latter the competition way. Both have value.

1a

2a

1 Stand with your left leg forward in front stance, guard in freestyle. Prior to kicking, visualize the target in your mind's eye and focus. You must keep the body as relaxed as possible until the point of impact.

2 Lift the right leg to the side, but don't lean – keep upright. Pull the kicking toes back and keep the supporting leg bent. It is common to lift up at this point, so check this and stay level. Lifting causes loss of balance and makes for a slower attack.

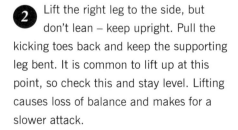

POINTS TO REMEMBER

• Be sure to twist the supporting leg as the kick strikes. This will allow you to use your hips as well as gain maximum range.

• There are many bones in the foot and this kick often collides with elbows, so train for accuracy to avoid injury.

• The instep needs to be conditioned for kicking, which is best done with a kick bag. Start hitting it lightly and make good contact with the flat surface of the foot. When you are happy with this, start to increase speed and power.

SIDE VIEW

Of all the kicks, Mawashi Geri is one of the hardest to break down into stages. You need to make it flow from beginning to end. It is vital that you twist the hips at the right time, otherwise the kick will be greatly weakened. Don't worry about height to start off with – try to develop a smooth action you can control. Note that your kicking foot should travel round in the same plane as your leg.

3a

3 Kick out with the right leg in a snapping action. At the same time, rotate the hips by twisting the rear foot 180 degrees, pivoting on the heel. Don't kick short of the target; when kicking to the head, for example, you should see your foot travel past your face. This way you know you are making a penetrating attack.

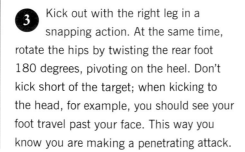

4 Snap the kicking leg back quickly. You now have the option of moving forward or stepping back. A common mistake with Mawashi Geri is to raise the heel from the floor to gain height; never do this, as you will only execute a weak attack of no value.

The spinning back kick is one of the most challenging kicks because it involves balancing on one leg as you spin, in addition to turning your back on your opponent momentarily. Because its delivery must be quick, timing is of the essence and you need a strong supporting leg. When successfully landed, this kick is one of the most powerful, as it uses the momentum of the spin and the driving hips. It is essential not to telegraph your intention to your opponent prior to and during the attack.

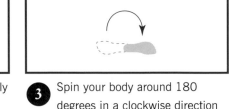

1 Step forward from yoi position into front stance, with your left leg forward and your guard held in freestyle. Just before you begin the kick, narrow your stance slightly to allow for a smoother spinning action. You are aiming to complete this whole technique in one fluid motion, without any pause.

2 Draw the kicking (rear) leg closely into the supporting leg, tucking your foot behind the knee. Keep the supporting leg flexed and the hips level – if you lock the supporting leg, or raise your hips, this increases the likelihood of losing your balance, while at the same time indicating to your opponent your intention to kick.

3 Spin your body around 180 degrees in a clockwise direction (the opposite way when kicking with the left leg), pivoting on your heel, keeping the kicking leg tightly wrapped around the supporting leg. Keep your hips level. It is vital that the spin derives from a strong turning action in the hips, and not from turning the shoulders. At the same time, turn your head to look over your shoulder at your opponent.

4 Keeping the supporting leg bent, drive your right leg out at the target, fully extending it. Don't let yourself lean either to the left or the right, as this will cause loss of balance at the critical moment of impact. Keep spinning as you kick out. When the kick is complete, you should finish back facing the direction you started at, having turned a full 360 degrees. Remember to recover the kick quickly, so that you don't leave yourself vulnerable to a counter-attack.

STRIKE AREA

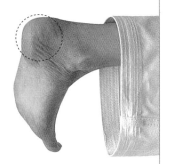

Strike with the heel – point your toes to the floor, flexing your foot to make it rigid. On impact, tense the ankle to absorb the blow.

COMMON MISTAKES

Take care not to overspin, taking your body round too far and kicking off line.

FRONT VIEW

Note that the body remains aligned as the kick is executed. The attacker maintains focus on her opponent with just one eye.

POINTS TO REMEMBER

• It is vital that the kick is delivered in the shortest possible time, as you are putting yourself at a disadvantage by turning your back on your opponent momentarily.

• From the moment your foot leaves the floor, make this attack in one fluid action. Any hesitation or added movement will indicate your intentions and give your opponent an opening.

第七課・総合型

Combination Work

The five combination sequences that you will find in this section are ones that I have taught in my lessons over the years. Some of them were taught to me by my instructors, and I am now passing them on in turn; others I have devised myself. That is one of the great things about karate: it should never be boring. A good instructor will always be thinking of new ways to teach the traditional basics. Each class should be an adventure.

You will find when you join a class that much of the combination work is based around the grading syllabus. This is fine in itself, and will help you prepare for your next belt. However, when I was progressing through the ranks, there was no set syllabus, and this meant that each examination had an element of surprise – no bad thing in an art form that advocates the development of an open mind, able to react to change rather than freeze in shock. So, don't just blinker your training to cope with the demands of a grading – karate is much more than this.

The following combinations are designed to test you by making you move in ways that standard class training may not offer. They are here to make you think and for you to practise, so you can spice up your training. The sequences take most of the basic blocks, punches, strikes and kicks and put them together in ways that will help you to develop a whole range of skills, including coordination, balance, the correct use of stance and more. The foot-position diagrams for each combination are grouped together, to make it easy to see – at a glance – how your feet move throughout each sequence.

As with all combination work, it is vital that you don't just concentrate on your 'good' side. Practise, so that in the end it is difficult to tell which side is which. Always try to make the sequence flow. The combination will have its own rhythm – work to it. Try to avoid hesitation, or missing out a movement completely. Imagine that every gap in the flow of movement is an opening for an opponent. Train to be fluid.

Kumite demands the ability to put all the basic movements you have learned into action. If you have trained hard in your combination work, you will find that your kumite flows more easily and will not break down so often. The link between the two is very strong, and it is not uncommon to find karate-ka taking two or three combinations that work for them in kumite, and practising them over and over again until they become second nature. It is only in this way – through constant repetition and years of training – that you can hope to develop a high degree of skill in the study of karate-do.

Combination A

This punch–block–punch–block combination is a simple way for a student to practise punching and blocking in a small area. The combination involves stepping, punching and blocking. Each move should involve a hip twist and good stance work. Take care not to rush and to complete each technique correctly before moving on.

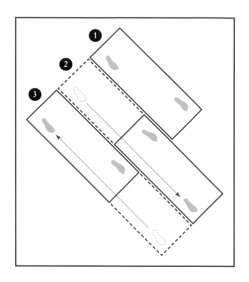

1 Stand in front stance, with your left leg forward in Gedan Barai block. Remember that, as you start to step, push off hard with the back leg.

POINTS TO REMEMBER

• Never lean to assist movement.

• When making reverse punch, keep your back straight and let the hips and chest create the power.

2 Step punch to the face (jodan). As you land, make sure your body is square on to the target. Check that your back leg is locked.

3 Now, pushing off with the right foot, step back into left leg front stance. At the same time as you land, make left arm rising block, Age Uke. Remember to twist the chest and hips to 45 degrees. When stepping backwards, don't lean the upper body to help speed up your step – use the leg muscles to propel you.

4 Now counter with reverse punch, Gyaku Zuki. As you punch, lock your back leg, rotate your hips and chest and pull the reaction hand back sharply. The torso should now be square on.

5 Finish the combination with left arm downward block, Gedan Barai. Don't move the hips too soon here. Take the blocking arm up in preparation, and only at the last moment, when you are about to complete the block, turn the hips to 45 degrees. As with all hip movements, the later you leave them the sharper your karate will become.

Combination B

This combination is designed to help develop the ability to change direction and stance. The techniques are not in themselves the issue. Later, when you are more familiar with the sequence, change the techniques around to avoid it becoming stale. A true karate-ka should be able to move and change direction with ease. Train to be fluid.

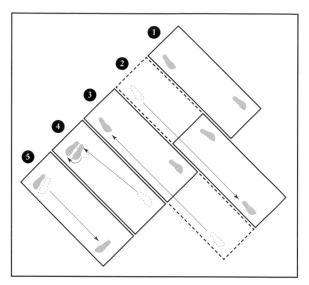

1 Stand in left leg front stance, Gedan Barai position. Again, remember to push off with the back leg when you step.

2 Step with the back leg and make stepping punch to the mid-section, Oi Zuki chudan. Remember to stay level – don't lift up in an effort to gain speed or power. Lock the legs on impact.

POINTS TO REMEMBER

• Step 4 is a midpoint. When attacking, only hold this position for a moment, then make the attack. As your skill increases, this midpoint will last a mere fraction of a second.

• Keep level. No extra power is gained by bouncing up and down.

• Keep as much tension as possible in the legs to create a power stance as you strike. Remember to turn your feet in and push your knees out. And don't lean back.

• When you deliver the strike, don't lift up – a common mistake. Stay low and push your hips and chest into it.

3 Now open the right palm, withdraw the left fist to the side of the face and, pushing off with the right heel, step back and make left arm outside block, Ude Uke. As you land, remember to twist the body to 45 degrees. The block should finish at the same time as the step. Remember: even though you have stepped back, you must thrust your weight forward on completion of the block. Keep the front knee well bent.

4 Prepare to strike with the elbow, Empi. Keeping your hips level, slide your left foot back to the right one, at the same time opening the blocking fist and stretching it away from you, palm up. Keep your face to your opponent and your shoulders down.

5 Now attack with the point of the elbow, Empi, sliding the left foot out into horse stance. Remain level. Only as the knees push out and you complete the stance should you strike with Empi. Note that the open hand has now become a fist and rotated on impact.

6 From this position, now strike with the back of the fist, Uraken. Once the attack is complete, snap it back as in position 5.

Combination C

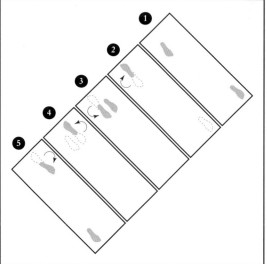

This combination appears difficult. It is. Use it to develop a high level of balance and hip flexibility. It doesn't really matter what kicks you use; try to mix them up and create problems for yourself.

1 Stand left leg forward in front stance, guard held in freestyle.

2 Keeping the back straight, lift the front foot and make left leg side thrust kick, Yoko Geri. Keep your face to the target and your arms and upper body relaxed.

POINTS TO REMEMBER

• Don't hold the fists too tightly as you kick. This will create tension and slow you down.

• When kicking off the front foot, don't lean back to help get the foot off the floor. Also, leave the back foot where it is – don't slide it in and make a shorter stance. That's cheating.

• The height of the kicks doesn't really matter at this stage. Get the technique right and worry about high kicks later.

• This is a difficult combination. Make it smooth and flowing, and try to avoid jerky movements.

3 Recover the kick, keeping a high knee lift, then drive the left foot down so it sits beside the right. Keep your knees bent. To complicate things, add a right arm Gedan Barai as you land. The block should finish at the same time as the foot hits the floor. Focus is vital, so be sure that the body tenses at this moment.

4 From this standing position, now quickly lift the right knee to the side and make round house kick, Mawashi Geri. Remember to pick your knee up as high as possible and not to lean away to get greater height. Snap your kick back, but keep your knee up.

5 Now drive the right knee down and make right leg front stance. At the same time as you land, push the left side of your body forwards and make left arm reverse punch, Gyaku Zuki.

Combination D

This combination uses kicks, blocks and strikes. Don't rush the initial attack so as to speed up the sequence. Finish each technique off as you would deal with an attacker, then move on. Remember: it's not the number of moves executed but the quality of each technique that exemplifies advanced karate.

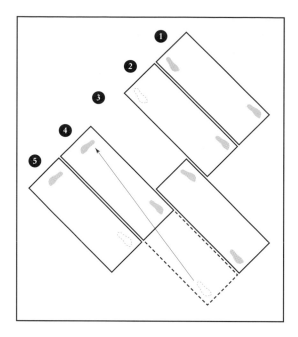

POINTS TO REMEMBER

• Keep the supporting leg bent when you kick. This will stop you lifting up when you kick and perhaps losing balance.

• When striking with rising elbow attack, keep the arm pressed tightly to the side of the head.

• Strike with the point of the elbow.

• Throughout the combination, keep face with your opponent.

1 Stand in front stance, left leg forward, guard held in freestyle.

2 Lift the right knee and attack with front kick, Mae Geri. Don't alter your guard or telegraph your intention by adding extra movements.

3 Recover the kick with a strong snapping action, hold your balance and then step forward into right leg front stance. As you land, deliver a rising elbow strike, Age Empi.

4 Pushing off through the right foot, step back with the right leg, making left leg back stance knife hand block, Shuto Uke. As you land, make sure that you have shifted your weight on to the rear leg and your heels are in line.

5 Focus your stance for a moment and check your balance. Now, without moving the rear leg, lift the front knee and kick left leg side thrust kick, Yoko Geri. Once the kick is finished, recover with a strong knee position and then step forward into front stance.

Combination E

This final combination is set to develop hip flexibility and balance as well as kicking accuracy. When kicking, always aim at a target. Don't fall into the trap of losing focus when practising basics – always imagine an opponent and strike a defined target; never lash out blindly.

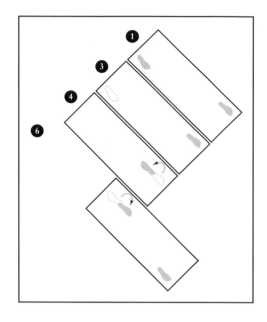

POINTS TO REMEMBER

• When attacking with knife hand strike, remember to keep the thumb well bent as this strengthens the wrist.

• When practising the change from front kick to back kick, allow yourself to stop at the midpoint to correct your balance. Later, as skill improves, try to make the sequence one fluid action.

1 Stand with your left leg forward in front stance, and your guard held in freestyle position.

2 Use your right hand to attack with knife hand strike, Shuto Uchi, to the side of the face. Push your chest and hips into the attack. To increase power, pull the reaction arm back strongly to the left hip.

3 Leave the striking arm out and deliver a right leg front kick, Mae Geri, to the mid-section. Don't drop the right arm as you kick: hold it focused in place – it's not easy.

4 Keeping the hips level and the supporting knee well bent, recover the front kick with a snapping action. At the same time rotate the body clockwise 180 degrees and wrap the right foot behind the left knee. You are now ready to attack with spinning back kick, Ushiro Geri. Make sure you maintain eye contact with your opponent even though you have your back to them.

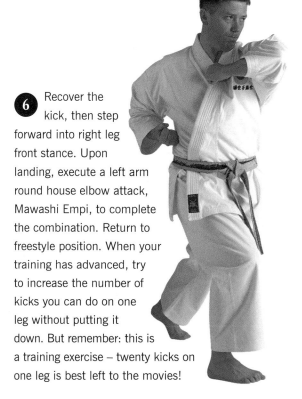

5 Drive the right heel out to the target, keeping the upper body relaxed. You often see Ushiro Geri executed to jodan, but chudan offers a greater target area, which is something to bear in mind. Lock the kicking knee strongly on impact.

6 Recover the kick, then step forward into right leg front stance. Upon landing, execute a left arm round house elbow attack, Mawashi Empi, to complete the combination. Return to freestyle position. When your training has advanced, try to increase the number of kicks you can do on one leg without putting it down. But remember: this is a training exercise – twenty kicks on one leg is best left to the movies!

第八課・組手

Sparring • Kumite

When you first start training, you will probably be keen to start fighting. This isn't such a good idea: your distance, timing and – most importantly – your control will not be of a high enough standard to be given free rein. For this very reason, stages of pre-arranged fighting were developed to allow keen new students the chance to practise attack and defence with a partner but with safety limits built in. As your skill improves, the restraints are relaxed, until you find yourself facing an opponent in free fighting with no set routine.

A range of fighting sequences is included on the following pages. The instructions are always directed to the defender, but there are tips for the attacker too. Regardless of the type of kumite, certain factors never change:

• **Spirit** No matter how tired you are, what injuries you may have or how much better your opponent may be, never give in. Fight until you are told to stop on the command *yame*.
• **Distance** Remember: too close, and you will have little or no time to react; too far away, and your counter will have little or no effect.
• **Timing** Being able to read and deal with a situation takes years of training and demands maximum concentration and willpower.

SANBON KUMITE

This three-step sparring introduces beginners to pairing-up work. The attacker announces the area he intends to attack, then delivers three attacks, one after the other, to that target. The defender blocks these, then counter-attacks after the third block. Attacker and defender then swap roles and start again.

IPPON KUMITE

This is the next stage. Here, the attacker still announces the target area but only delivers one attack, and the defender blocks and counters immediately. By this point, the defender will have numerous blocks and counters at hand, making his kumite quite inventive.

JIYU IPPON KUMITE

This is the last stage before freestyle proper. To make things more difficult for the defender, the attacker now moves around feinting, probing for an opening. Both attacker and defender must now start to develop tactics that will help them in free fighting.

JIYU KUMITE / FREE FIGHTING

For most students, this is what it's all about. Here you are given the chance to experiment. There are rules, but these are for safety and don't hinder you from developing a style of fighting that works for you. Never become complacent – always push yourself harder, try new things, don't be afraid to look silly. Fight everyone you can at every opportunity and build up a reservoir of experience.

In three-step sparring, both attacker and defender have a role to play. When you attack, make sure that your opponent has to block. When you block, make sure the block works. At the point of counter-punching, use maximum force and intent but make sure you control the technique; if you don't, it will finish your opponent. It is for good reason that Ippon is often referred to as 'the killing blow'.

DEFENDER　　　　　ATTACKER

1 Stand upright in yoi, ready stance. The attacker stands in left leg front stance. Make sure you are standing close enough for there to be a real chance that the attacker will step in and land his punch. Learning the importance of distance is vital.

2 The attacker steps and punches to the face with the right arm. At the same time, you retreat and make rising block, Age Uke. Make sure you block wrist to wrist.

POINTS TO REMEMBER

• On each occasion of blocking, the defender must rotate his body to 45 degrees to reduce the target area offered to the attacker. This is vital in preparation for the counter-attack.

3 The attacker again makes stepping punch to the face, this time with the left arm. Step back and make right arm rising block.

4 The attacker makes his last stepping punch to the face. Step back and block with your left arm. At this point, you should both check that you are close enough to make an effective counter.

5 Now counter-attack with right hand reverse punch, Gyaku Zuki. Aim for the solar plexus. Be sure that the hips and chest are timed with the strike. As you hit the target, make a strong kiai.

The same rule applies here as in jodan: correct distance at all times. The attacker should never feel that he can't reach, and the defender should never escape so far that he cannot counter the moment an opening occurs. Even though this sparring sequence is taught as the most basic form of partner work, done correctly it can be extremely challenging. For example, the attacker shouldn't always attack at the same speed or in the same rhythm. And, as for the defender – sometimes stand a little closer than usual to cut down your reaction time and create a little more pressure for yourself. Training must push you to the limit if it is to have any value.

1 Stand in yoi ready position. The attacker stands in front stance, left leg forward. The attacker calls 'chudan', announcing the target area.

DEFENDER   ATTACKER

2 The attacker steps forward and makes chudan stepping punch – Oi Zuki – to the mid-section. Step back with your left leg and block with your right arm, outside block (Ude Uke).

102

3 The attacker advances again, punching to the mid-section. Step back with the right leg this time, and make outside block with the left arm.

4 The attacker makes the last stepping attack. Retreat with the left leg and again make outside block with the right arm. On all three blocks, attempt to use a strong twisting action in the wrist, to help deflect the attack as much as possible.

5 Slide your right foot back and at the same time prepare to attack with elbow strike, Empi, using the right elbow. Remember to keep level as you slide out and to keep your face to your opponent.

6 Now strike to the attacker's solar plexus, pushing out with the right leg into horse stance. As you strike the target, tense the legs strongly to absorb the impact. Remember to use kiai.

一本組手上段

The distance needed to block is not always the same as that required to counter. In this sequence the defender has to make a stance change to allow the use of the kick. Getting this right takes years of practice – start slowly and work on fluid movement.

1 Stand in yoi, ready stance. The attacker stands in left leg front stance. The onus is on the attacker to check that he is close enough to make an effective attack (in other words, one that has to be blocked).

DEFENDER   ATTACKER

2 The attacker shouts 'jodan' and then makes stepping punch to the head. Step back with the right leg and make left arm rising block, Age Uke.

POINTS TO REMEMBER

• As with all combinations, try to make sure everything runs smoothly, with no gaps in the flow of events.

• No block, no counter. If you don't block properly you won't be in a position to carry on, let alone make your own counter-attacks.

Now slide your front foot back to create the correct distance to counter with a kick to the head. Remember to keep your back straight. In order to weaken your opponent, pull him off balance by holding his punching arm and pulling him forward.

Deliver a right leg round house kick, Mawashi Geri, to the side of the face. You can use the ball of the foot or the instep – bear in mind that using the instep increases the reach of the kick and is safer than the ball of the foot, so it's probably best to use this to start off with. Having countered, snap the kick back sharply, then return your leg to the floor as quickly as possible. Always be in a position to carry on the fight.

In this sequence the attacker counters with spear hand, or Nukite. Great care must be taken with open-hand techniques as they can easily damage the eyes – one of the reasons for keeping nails cut short! Spear hand is an often neglected attack, but none the less a very real one when it strikes the intended target area.

1 Stand in yoi, ready stance. The attacker stands in front stance, left leg forward. Attacker: don't look down or away. Develop the confidence to look directly at your opponent and let him know you mean business.

DEFENDER   ATTACKER

2 The attacker shouts 'chudan' then makes stepping punch to the mid-section. Step back with the right leg and make left arm downward sweeping block, Gedan Barai.

POINTS TO REMEMBER

• This attack is only suitable for extremely vulnerable soft areas of the body, such as the throat or eyes. If you were to strike with spear hand to a hard target area, you would most likely cause damage to your hand.

STRIKE AREA

It is said that spear hand was developed in order for a karate-ka to be able to defend himself against an opponent wearing armour. The spear hand would be aimed at the joints in the armour where narrow targets presented themselves. Today it is most commonly seen in kata, but is still a valid weapon when aimed at the eyes, throat or solar plexus. To execute it correctly demands years of conditioning, so don't try this technique until you feel confident in your karate. A strong wrist is vitally important to avoid the hand buckling on impact.

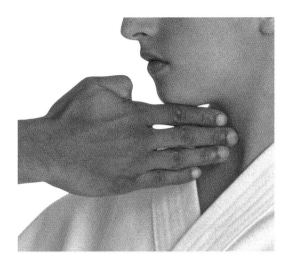

3 You now counter with right hand Nukite to the attacker's throat. The attack should be accompanied by the rotation of the chest and hips and feel similar to reverse punch in execution. Be sure to pull the reaction arm back at speed to assist the attack.

Here the defender is given the opportunity to counter with two hand techniques: one to the face, one to the body. Train to make the delay between counters as small as possible. You will find when training that many students, for whatever reason (though usually pain), kick off target. Don't allow this, or you won't know if your blocks are working. Always aim for the target.

POINTS TO REMEMBER

• The more you unbalance your opponent with your block, the less chance they will be in a position to fight back, and the longer you have to counter-attack.

• Block as strongly as possible; the pain this inflicts often softens up an opponent and weakens their resolve.

• It's not easy to find the solar plexus under a karate gi, so find your own using a prod of your finger and apply this knowledge to your opponent. It is used as a target area because, unlike the stomach muscles, it can't be built up. You will know when you hit it!

DEFENDER   ATTACKER

1 Stand in yoi, ready stance. The attacker stands in left leg front stance, guard held in freestyle. Attacker: remember that your legs are longer than your arms, so don't stand too close!

2 The attacker shouts 'Mae Geri' then attacks with a right leg front kick to the stomach. As she attacks, step back with the right leg and make left arm downward block, Gedan Barai. As you block, try to knock the attacker off balance so that she is disorientated for a moment.

3 As the attacker lands with her right leg forward, draw your left fist to the side of your face and then counter with back fist strike, Uraken Uchi, to the attacker's jaw.

4 The moment the strike lands, counter with reverse punch, Gyaku Zuki, to the solar plexus. Make sure you make full use of the chest and hips on the reverse punch, and maintain maximum focus (kime) as the punch lands.

In this sequence the defender uses a step with the right leg combined with a left arm block not only to parry the attack but also to help draw the attacker on to the counter. This is easier said than done and requires great skill. Remember also that the attacker's head will be meeting the counter-kick, so watch your control. The golden rule is that if you are close enough to hit, you are also close enough to be hit.

DEFENDER   ATTACKER

1 Stand in yoi, ready stance. The attacker stands in front stance, left leg forward, guard held in freestyle.

2 The attacker shouts 'Mae Geri', then delivers a front snap kick to the stomach. At the same time, step out with your right leg and make downward block, Gedan Barai, with your left arm. This step takes you away from the attack, so if the block were to fail, the attacker would kick thin air as opposed to your ribs. This is a good opportunity to knock the attacker off balance.

110

3 Now attack to the head with left leg side thrust kick, Yoko Geri. Remember to lock the leg but to aim a fraction short of the target for safety. If you are not that confident kicking to the head, then attack to the body.

4 As the leg recovers, step forward into front stance and attack with round house elbow strike, Mawashi Empi, to the solar plexus. Drive the hips and chest into the attack for maximum effect.

POINTS TO REMEMBER

• Kicks are generally heavy and hard to block. Don't rely on brute strength to defeat them. Always attempt to get your body out of the way just in case.

• If you can take the attacker off balance when you block, all the better, as this will create a window of opportunity for you to counter.

• As with all combination counters, work slowly to start with: make it work, then apply the speed. Be sure to return the kicking foot to the floor at speed, but don't rush and thus make the kick less effective.

横蹴けこみ

This block and counter works just as well whether the attacker kicks to the face or body. Attempt to use the block to spin your opponent round, thus exposing the kidneys and spine. You need maximum attention to control when attacking these areas. As a rule, the legs are heavier and stronger than the arms, so don't rely too heavily on the block. Make sure you step away quickly to avoid the kick.

1 Stand in yoi, ready stance. The attacker stands in front stance, left leg forward, guard held in freestyle.

DEFENDER　　　　ATTACKER

POINTS TO REMEMBER

• Attacker: try to develop a side thrust kick that isn't easily deflected. Use a partner to try to knock you off balance as you kick – it works wonders.

• As with all combinations, work to a point where there is no gap between the fist hitting the target and the foot the leaving the floor to strike to chudan.

• When you kick remember that you have the choice of using the instep or ball of the foot. Practise with both.

• When blocking the attack, attempt to spin the attacker so that he has his back to you. This gives you a large target area and stops him from blocking your counter.

2 Attacker shouts 'Yoko Geri', then attacks with a mid-section side thrust kick using the side edge of the foot. Step back with your right leg and, just as the attacker's kick is locking out, block with a left arm outside block, Ude Uke. Time this movement so that the blocking arm connects with the ankle.

3 As the attacker lands you should find that he has his back to you. Now counter with right hand reverse punch, Gyaku Zuki. You have two obvious target areas: kidneys and spine. Be careful.

4 Now recover your hands to freestyle position and at the same time lift your right leg and counter with round house kick, Mawashi Geri, to the body. Stay low as you kick and you will avoid the attacker's guard. After you hit the target, snap the foot back and step away from the attacker.

横蹴けこみ

In this sequence the defender puts together a foot then a hand counter. The most important thing to get right is making sure the initial block works. Remember: no block, no counter.

DEFENDER   ATTACKER

POINTS TO REMEMBER

• When kicking off the front foot, don't lean back to assist the knee lift, as this will weaken the kick.

• If you find yourself too far away to kick after blocking, make up the distance by sliding up the back foot. Remember to keep level, though.

• It's important to get the timing of the block right: catch the ankle, not the back of the leg.

1 Stand in yoi, ready stance, with the attacker in left leg front stance, guard held in freestyle.

2 The attacker calls 'Yoko Geri', then attacks with a right leg side thrust kick to the mid-section. You react to this by stepping back with the right leg and blocking the kick with left arm outside block, Ude Uke.

3 As the attacker lands, now counter-attack with side thrust kick to the mid-section. Here the kick will be with the left leg, coming off the front foot. Remember to strike with the edge of the foot and to lock the leg. Think about driving the kick through your opponent.

4 Now recover the kicking leg and step forward into front stance, at the same time striking to the side of the head with knife hand strike, Shuto Uchi. Don't forget to twist the striking hand on impact, and to be aware of good control when attacking this vulnerable point.

In this combination the defender again has to deal with a kick, but then counters using a popular self-defence technique: the palm heel strike. A new problem raises its head here in that a round house kick – because of its circular route to the target – follows the defender as he attempts to step inside it. Consequently, timing the step and block correctly is vital.

DEFENDER   ATTACKER

1 Stand in yoi, ready stance. The attacker steps forward into left leg front stance, guard held in freestyle.

2 The attacker shouts 'Mawashi Geri', then attacks with a right leg round house kick to the mid-section, chudan. As she does so, step back with your right leg and block with left arm downward block, Gedan Barai. Make sure to connect on the shin just above the ankle.

POINTS TO REMEMBER

• Keep the wrist strong – it's easy to injure the joint.

• Remember to apply basic principles when attacking, such as hip and chest rotation and maximum use of kime.

• Don't rush these attacks – make sure you are hitting the correct target and can control the technique.

3 As the attacker lands, counter with right arm palm heel strike, Teisho Uchi, to the jaw. Remember to keep the wrist well bent and to strike with the heel of the hand. Take care with control.

4 Now roll the wrist over and strike to the eyes with the fingers. Keep the thumb well bent and avoid the mouth. Do this movement slowly, pushing the head back at the same time. This is real self-defence, and not seen in normal practice. As a rule, these attacks should only be taught to more advanced students, who can deliver such counter-attacks with accuracy and control.

In this sequence the defender has to avoid a Mawashi Geri. The golden rule here is always try to get inside a round house kick: this will prevent the attacker penetrating your guard, while at the same time opening up the attacker to a counter.

POINTS TO REMEMBER

• Hitting someone in the stomach can wind them. This will tend to bring the head forward rather sharply; if you are then countering to the face, be aware of this and be sure to control your counter.

• When making inside block against Mawashi Geri, don't step back in a straight line – step off to 45 degrees. This will get you out of the way and create a bigger target area for when you counter.

DEFENDER   ATTACKER

1 Stand in yoi, ready stance, with the attacker left leg forward in front stance, guard held in freestyle.

2 The attacker shouts 'Mawashi Geri jodan' then attacks with a round house kick to the head. At the same time, step back with your right leg and make left arm inside block, Uchi Uke.

3 As the attacker lands, slide the front foot back and counter-attack with round house kick to the mid-section. Make contact with the ball of the foot, and try to hit the solar plexus if you can.

4 Once you have snapped the kick back, step into your opponent and strike to the face with back fist strike, Uraken. This is a very fast, snapping attack and it's easy to leave the hips and chest out while you execute it. Don't.

後
蹴

Due to the fact that back kick is a fast, strong attack, it does pose problems for a defender. If you aren't switched on, you will find that the kick has already hit you before you have time to react. Stay alert and, the moment the attacker spins, step out of the way.

DEFENDER   ATTACKER

1 Stand in yoi, ready stance, with the attacker in left leg front stance, guard held in freestyle. Attacker: don't make your stance too wide or it will slow the spin.

2 The attacker calls 'Ushiro Geri', then spins and attacks with back kick to the mid-section. Step back with your right leg and make downward block, Gedan Barai, with the left arm. Don't step back in line with the kick but step out at an angle of 45 degrees, so taking your body off line. This angle change is vital in creating a target area to strike at when you counter.

Now attack with front kick, Mae Geri, to the attacker's mid-section. Remember to stay low and to drive both hips into the kick. Your earlier body-shift to 45 degrees has now opened up the attacker's centre line and you have a choice of target areas. The throat, stomach and groin are now all vulnerable.

As the front kick snaps back, drive forward into front stance. As you land, attack with rising elbow strike, Age Empi, to the jaw.

POINTS TO REMEMBER

• Once you have the sequence worked out, attempt to block the back kick and then counter with your own kick without delay. The attacker should be knocked off balance and then hit as he lands. Give him no time to react.

• When you counter-attack with front kick, the blow may bring the attacker's head forward in an involuntary movement. This is good, but remember that as the head comes forward, your elbow strike must be executed with great control. Empi is a very powerful attack, so beware.

発展

Part Three
Taking it Further

In this section we look at kata in greater detail, and hopefully explain some of its mysteries. We also look at ways of keeping things fresh, and training in different areas of the art. Even if you have already been training for some time, there should be points here that are new to you – or at the very least might prompt a long-lost memory. I have tried to give advice based on my own experiences in the hope that you will put it to good use. Every teacher has their own way, and I am no different, but when writing this book I decided to put into words advice passed on to me by my instructors, all of whom – even now, twenty years on – I still have the utmost respect for, and still train under today. Everyone has a teacher.

Keeping Your Training Fresh

You should now be training regularly at your local club. You may even have graded. It should by this point be apparent to you that karate isn't just about learning a series of movements and hitting people. How, then, do you keep your training fresh? My advice is to set yourself goals, such as getting the next belt, improving your kata or working on your flexibility. Something else you can do is spice up your training. Below are a few examples, but there are many more things you can do.

COMPETITION

For me, karate has to be real. By this I mean it has to *work*. I am not suggesting visiting the local bar and taking on all-comers – these misinformed individuals have missed the point! The maxim 'Karate begins and ends with courtesy' appears sadly lacking in cases such as this. So, how do you know if it works? Well, the one way of testing yourself today is by entering a competition. It can be at local club level, a regional tournament or a national championship. It doesn't really matter. What is important is that you are testing yourself.

At this point I should say that many karate-ka past and present have argued against competition, stating that an art so deadly is watered down by introducing rules and scoring. I can see their point. Karate can be a dangerous pastime; it teaches mental and physical discipline – a martial code where injury and pain are discounted. How, then, is it possible for this 'way of the warrior' to incorporate a pastime in which competitors win trophies and score points? Speaking as someone who competed for fourteen years as a junior and senior, then retired from the competition mat, the truth is, it can. Competition karate does have rules, but then again boxing had the Marquess of Queensberry, and no one can claim that this Western martial art is diminished by his intervention. It is a part of human nature to want to compete, to challenge one another, and the obvious progression of this is the competition mat.

I have heard it said by somewhat misinformed commentators that competition fighting weakens the karate-ka, as it inhibits fighters to working on only a small number of safe techniques. Let me state, for the record, that many of the true greats of modern karate have been both traditionalists and competitors. Sensei Enoeda, the Shotokan 'tiger' renowned throughout the world for his mastery of karate, was the karate champion of Japan. In the modern era, Sensei Frank Brennan – probably the most technically gifted karate-ka of his generation, and a role model to a generation of students – was a fantastic competitor, taking karate to a new dimension. Sensei Brennan's achievement was that he combined a wonderfully exciting fighting style with an unflappable calm. A true warrior and gentleman …

This is why I advocate competition karate, because at its best it allows the karate-ka the opportunity to display virtues that are sadly lacking in society: courage, determination, self-control and true sincerity. The two strands should be able to co-exist, and that's the point of competition. It doesn't matter if you win or lose; what matters is that you gave your all.

BAG WORK

An area sadly neglected by karate-ka is impact work, better known as hitting the bag. As a junior grade I had never hit a punchbag until I visited the Red Triangle dojo in Liverpool, England. Here, Sensei Andy Sherry 7th Dan introduced me to the 'heavy bag'. I quickly learned which techniques I threw worked and which did not. During the morning classes we all wore training shoes – no one said why, but I decided it was for extra weight on the legs, which helped to condition muscles as well as to protect the feet, as the heavy bag felt like it was filled with bricks. The use of a bag is vital. It teaches you what it feels like to hit with full power and the effects this has on balance, stance, distance and timing. It is also extremely tiring and an excellent way of

Here we see two fighters battling it out on the mat. Note the use of hand mitts for protection. Many styles of karate now demand that fighters wear padding on their fists to reduce injury – not a move I necessarily advocate, as I believe it can lead to the development of poor control.

working out. Use it to supplement your training: if your dojo doesn't have one, put one up in your garage or find somewhere else suitable. Then, when you have a free moment, pop out and work out.

MAKIWARA

Another method of testing the power of your technique is to strike the makiwara. A makiwara is a striking board traditionally covered in straw, but nowadays usually a thick layer of rubber. The striking pad is attached to a sprung board which allows it to absorb the blows it receives. If you look at the hands of karate-ka who train with the makiwara, you will see the difference to those who don't. Callouses develop on the striking areas, hardening them over a period of time and making them formidable weapons. Today, few people use such extreme training methods, but many karate-ka still swear by its use. Personally, I have used them and would say it's not for everybody, and certainly not the young. If you intend to have a go, expect a degree of pain and not a little blood.

SEMINARS

Every year the major associations in each country hold summer camps. These can be on university campuses or in holiday parks. I have attended many in my time, and I thoroughly suggest you do too. These courses usually have a number of very senior instructors teaching over a period of a few days, and they are an excellent way to invigorate your training. They can be truly inspiring, and show you what can be achieved with a lot of effort and years of dedication. You will also make new friends, and this is the great thing about karate: its language is universal. It is a wonderful way to break down barriers of race and religion.

平
安
四
段

Kata

There are roughly fifty kata being used in modern karate. Some of these are relatively new in origin, though many have been handed down from past generations. Each kata has its own name and set sequence of movements, although to stress the self-defence aspect of karate the first movement of each kata is always a block.

The aim of kata is to allow a karate-ka the opportunity to practise blocks, kicks, punches and strikes against a series of imaginary opponents. You will find the practice of kata challenging, as many movements are only to be found in the kata themselves and not in the basic movements of karate.

The initial kata a student will learn are compulsory and closely linked with the grading system. However, as your standard improves you will find that there are also more advanced kata that are optional. Here, students will select favoured kata to work on – depending on their own personal choice – be it for a grading, competition or just for the challenge. There are many to choose from, according to one's preference: some are designed to build strength and stamina; others, speed and dexterity.

The effects of practice are cumulative, so little and often is a good rule of thumb. Because the kata can be practised alone or as part of a group, they allow the karate-ka the opportunity to train outside of the dojo, be it in the garage or in a field. It doesn't really matter – what counts is that you practise the kata regularly.

PERFORMING KATA

Something you will discover for yourself as your training develops is that no matter how confident you become in the practice of basic movements and their application in kumite, the ability to perform kata to a high level evades most people. Why is this? I believe that to perform kata well, one not only has to develop technique of the highest standard but also has to learn how to control the mind.

The most common mistakes tend to be rushing or forgetting a move or sequence. This can almost always be blamed on a weak attitude. To combat this, the moment you make yoi and announce the kata, your mind should be set. Remain calm but alert. Put maximum effort into each movement as well as maintaining the correct mental attitude. Remember: you are not just hitting with your body – make sure your spirit comes through in everything you do. The more you practise kata, the more you allow your mind and body the opportunity to become familiar with the kata, and thereby store it in your memory.

TAKE IT SLOWLY

Don't try to learn too many kata straight away. A good instructor will make sure you learn each one at the appropriate stage in your development. A good method of learning a kata is to break it down into its main sequences and then, taking them one at a time, attempt to master them. This way you don't have to go all the way through to practise, and can take a sequence of a few movements and work on it until it is smooth and strong. Then, once you have done this, link it to the next sequence, which you have also practised in this way, and you will slowly build up the kata from beginning to end. Later, if you find you are having a problem with any part of the kata, single out that sequence and rework it.

NERVES

I don't know many people who are not nervous about performing kata – probably because it often means getting up on your own or as part of a small group. This is a rational fear, but not one you should give into. For starters, how can we say that we train in karate-do and at the same time admit that we can't do kata through nerves? OK, so you are nervous, but remember that everyone else is as well. Whether in a grading or a competition, the feeling is the same, so you need

to accept it and get on with it. Often the people who claim they don't like kata are the ones who cannot come to terms with this fear.

As a junior national kata champion, I can speak from experience when I say that I was terrified of getting up in front of an audience to perform, but I used to view it as a mental test and something that I should face. Sometimes it went well, others not, but at least I tried, and you can't ask for more than that. Never forget the karate adage: karate is not about winning or losing, but is about developing the character through training.

Don't, then, neglect your kata training. It is as much a part of your karate as the basics and kumite. When you are younger it is not uncommon to lean towards kumite, and that's fine – so did I. But just remember: we don't remain young warriors for ever.

RULES OF KATA

1. ORDER Each kata has a set sequence of movements, and a karate-ka must complete the kata in the correct order.
2. ACCURACY The starting position and the final movement of the kata are the same. A student must practise to return to the same spot every time. This is called *embusen*. Failure to do so usually points to incorrect use of stance.
3. UNDERSTANDING As stated earlier, there are many movements in each kata that are unique to that kata and have their own application. It is not enough just to be able to perform a movement; you should be able to apply it as well.
4. KIAI Most kata have two kiai: one in the middle of the kata, and one at the end. These are two focal points in the kata and must not be missed.
5. RHYTHM AND TIMING Each kata has a time to be completed – don't rush and finish too fast. By the same token, don't draw the kata out, making a performance of it. Take your time, and finish each movement with strength and the correct attitude.

HEIAN YONDAN

The kata demonstrated on the following pages is one from the Shotokan system called Heian Yondan. This kata is the fourth of the five Heian kata, and is taught for the purple-belt examination.

It is made up of twenty-seven moves (although I have broken it down into more steps on the following pages, to aid demonstration) and should take approximately fifty seconds to complete. It is one of the more aesthetically pleasing kata of the Heian group, combining strong, slow, graceful movements with subtle stance changes and shifting of balance.

Training in this kata introduces the karate-ka to open-hand blocks, open-hand strikes and even a jumping attack – movements not often touched on in basic training. It is not the aim of this section to teach kata, but rather to introduce new students to the concept of kata training. Stick to the golden rules *(see box left)* and you can't go far wrong – whatever kata you are learning. Remember to keep level throughout the sequence – always move on the same plane – and maintain a state of zanshin. And remember: a little, and often, will aid development in this area.

NOTE

Kata generally involve a number of changes in the direction you are facing. The steps for Heian Yondan on the following pages have been broken down into sections, relating to the direction you face when you actually perform the kata. However, in the interests of clarity, all the moves are shown from the front view, and therefore the arrow included at the beginning of each section shows the actual direction of orientation.

平安四段

SECTION ONE

The first part of the kata (moves 1–26) is performed facing forwards. The first of the two kiais is made on move 26, which marks the middle of the kata.

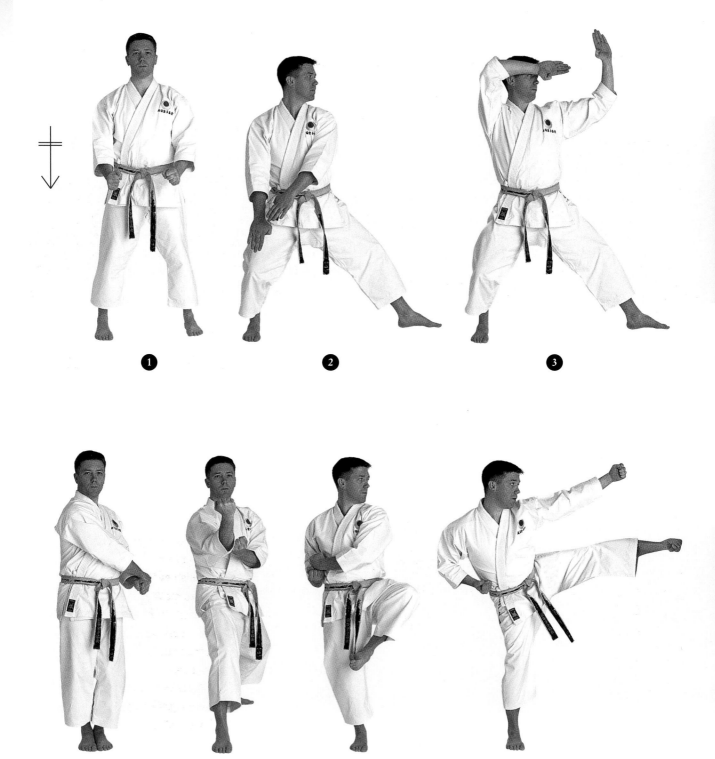

4　　　　5　　　　6　　　　7

12

13

KATA TIPS

- Make sure you remain level throughout.
- Finish each stance correctly before moving on.
- Even with the slow movements, make sure they are strong and carried out with the correct attitude.
- At move 7, make sure you leave a gap for the kick when you make x-block.

平安四段

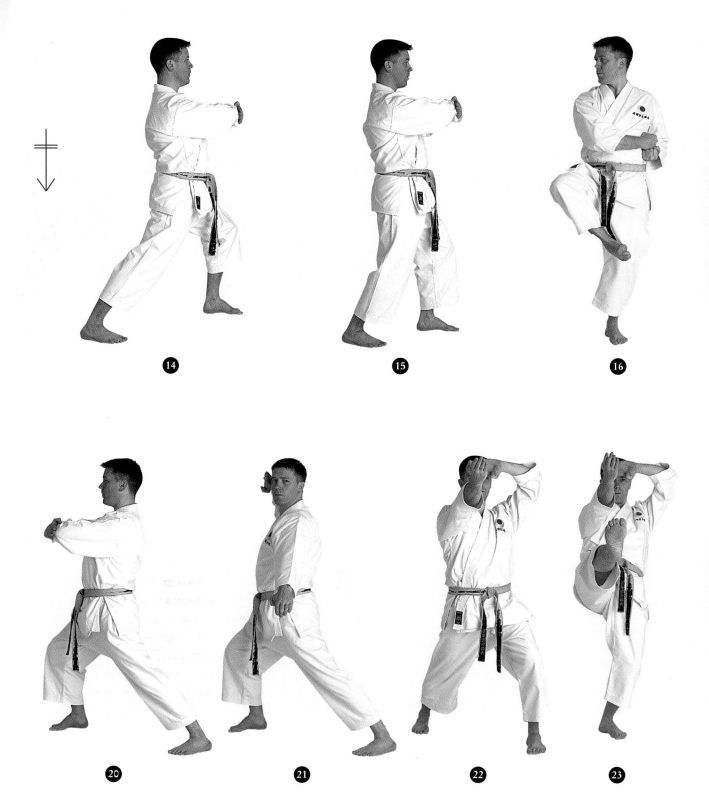

⓮

⓯

⓰

⓴

㉑

㉒

㉓

KIAI

KATA TIPS

• Recover the kick correctly, and this will give you time to make a strong Uraken attack.
• After attacking with front kick in move 23, don't drop your knee.
• In move 26, be sure to strike and make a kiai as you land, not after.

平安四段

SECTION TWO

This section (moves 27–31) is performed facing backwards, having turned the body to an angle of 45 degrees to the left of the centre line.

KATA TIPS

• To change direction, slide the left foot out at 45 degrees behind you, spinning on the right heel and turning your body, drawing your arms up to prepare for the block.
• When making double-hand block (move 27), don't let your elbows stick out. Keep them pulled in, under control.
• When you kick (move 29) don't lift up out of your stance. Stay level.

27

28

SECTION THREE

This next section (moves 32–36) is also performed facing backwards, but this time at an angle of 45 degrees to the right of the centre line.

KATA TIPS

• Pivot on your left heel to take you round to face 45 degrees right of the centre line.
• These moves are the exact opposite of section two, so the same rules apply. Keep level, and keep your elbows under control.

32

33

29

30

31

34

35

36

平安四段

SECTION FOUR

The last part of the kata (moves 37–45) is done facing the opposite direction to which you started. You should finish at the point where you began.

KATA TIPS

• When 'grabbing the head' in move 40, make sure your hands are level with your own head.

• In move 41, when striking with the knee remember to pull the hands down with kime to closed fists. As you strike with the knee, make a kiai.

37

38

42

43

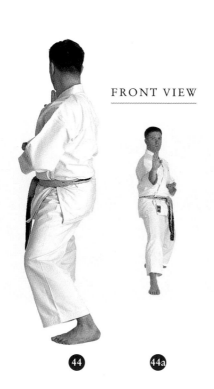

FRONT VIEW

44   **44a**

39

40

KIAI

41

45

KATA TIPS

• In move 42, turn 180 degrees by pivoting round to the left, on your left heel, bringing you round to face the direction in which you started. The remaining moves are now carried out facing this direction.

• At move 45 (yame – the finishing position) you should be at the same point at which you began.

The Dojo Code

Below is the dojo code – a set of statements embodying the essence of karate. Its aim is to unify the class so that each student – no matter what their ability – strives towards the same goal.

The code is chanted in Japanese at the end of a class by all the students present. Sadly, today it is rarely used in dojo outside Japan. Why this is I don't know. It seems silly that if we continue with bowing, wearing white gi and using Japanese terminology, we should have discarded the code that emphasizes all that is good about karate. The qualities it embodies – perseverance, fortitude, determination, self-control – are all ones that good instructors attempt to pass on to their students in any case.

The first Japanese instructors who came to the West had one aim in mind: to spread karate. They thought – and rightly – that an art which teaches students a superb form of self-defence, as well as a physical activity that refined the mind and body, would have far-reaching positive effects on those who fell under its spell. Unfortunately, the standards of karate taught today vary, and are sometimes driven more by financial motivation than by a desire to spread true karate. Therefore it is important to do the following when beginning your karate training: find a true karate-ka to teach you true karate-do. If you do this, then even if your club does not chant the code, it will be alive in you anyway.

Hitotsu! Jinkaku Kansei ni Tsutomuru Koto!

One! To strive for the perfection of character!

•

Hitotsu! Makoto No Michi O Mamoru Koto!

One! To defend the paths of truth!

•

Hitotsu! Doryoko No Seishin O Yashinau Koto!

One! To foster the spirit of effort!

•

Hitotsu! Reigi O Omonzuru Koto!

One! To honour the principles of etiquette!

•

Hitotsu! Kekki No Yu O Imashimuru Koto!

One! To guard against impetuous courage!

Final Words

So, there you have it – my guide for those of you new to karate, as well as those of you already in training who may be seeking further guidance. The views and opinions expressed are my own, formed over twenty years of karate experience.

As my wife Jacqueline (a 2nd Dan) pointed out, things that I take for granted could well be things a student has never heard before. And that is one of the great things about putting karate knowledge into print: the very fact that you have to sit down and think about each technique – how to explain it through the written word, as opposed to demonstrating it in front of a class. This challenge throws up a whole new perspective on karate study. I was reminded of a class I attended, where the instructor, Andy Sherry 7th Dan, explained that it is not enough just to sweat – anyone can do that. To make real progress in your karate, you have to study it, and think about even the tiniest details.

This book is by no means the definitive word on karate. There are many kicks, punches and blocks, for example, as well as kata, that I have omitted to mention. Why? Because, to my mind, if you wish to practise good karate, it is all about getting the basics right. Learn a technique, understand how it works, and refine it through repetition upon repetition. *Apply* it, so that it works. When you have done this, you will be on the right track. Enjoy your training – not for medals or belts, but for the well-being it will give you.

Much is written today relating to the spiritual benefits of practising martial arts. Indeed, karate was first promoted with the aim of developing the character through training: note the order of events! You cannot come to karate seeking a 'quick fix'. If something has value, it isn't cheaply bought or quickly gained. If you train sincerely, with the correct attitude, and stick with it, changes will occur – but they will creep up on you slowly. As your karate matures, so will you.

Finally, let's return to the dojo code. Sincerity, perseverance, loyalty – all these qualities manifest themselves through hard training. To put things in the right order: train hard and keep on training hard, and see what happens. So, then, I hope you enjoy the book – whatever your grade or style. I believe it has something to offer. Good luck with your training.

'Oss'

Glossary

Japanese	Pronunciation	English
Age Empi	ah-geh en-pee	Rising elbow strike
Age Uke	ah-geh oo-kay	Rising block
Budo	boo-do	Martial ways
Choku Zuki	cho-koo zoo-key	Straight punch
Chudan	chew-dahn	Chest area
Dachi	dah-chee	Stance
Dan	dahn	Black-belt grade level
Do	dough	The way of
Dojo	dough-joe	Training hall
Empi	en-pee	Elbow
Empi Uchi	en-pee oo-chee	Elbow strike
Gedan	geh-dahn	Lower body area
Gedan Barai	geh-dahn baa-rah-ee	Downward block
Geri	geh-rhee	Kick
Gi	ghee	Karate suit
Gohon Kumite	go-hon koo-me-teh	Five-step sparring
Gyaku	gya-koo	Reverse
Gyaku Zuki	gya-koo zoo-key	Reverse Punch
Hachiji Dachi	hah-chee-gee dah-chee	Open-leg stance
Haito	hi-toe	Ridge hand
Haito Uchi	hi-toe oo-chee	Ridge hand strike
Haiwan	hi-wahn	Back arm
Hanmi	hahn-me	Half-facing position
Hara	hah-rah	Concept of spiritual centre
Heian	hey-un	Peaceful mind
Heian Shodan	hey-un sho-dahn	'Peaceful mind' 1st level (formal exercise)
Heian Nidan	hey-un knee-dahn	2nd level
Heian Sandan	hey-un sun-dahn	3rd level
Heian Yondan	hey-un yon-dahn	4th level
Heian Godan	hey-un go-dahn	5th level
Heisoku Dachi	hey-sock-oo dah-chee	Informal attention stance
Hidari	he-dah-rhee	Left
Hiraken	he-rah-ken	Fore-knuckle fist
Hiza	he-zar	Knee
Ippon Kumite	ee-pon koo-me-teh	One-step sparring
Jiyu Ippon Kumite	gee-you ee-pon koo-me-teh	Semi-free one-step sparring
Jiyu Kumite	gee-you koo-me-teh	Freestyle sparring
Jodan	joe-dahn	Face area
Juji Uke	jew-gee oo-kay	X-block
Ka	kah	Person/practitioner
Kakato	kah-kah-toe	Heel
Karate	kah-rah-teh	Empty-hand fighting
Kata	kah-tah	Formal exercise
Keage	kay-ah-geh	Snap
Kebanashi	kay-bah-nah-she	Snap kick
Kekomi	kay-koh-me	Thrust kick
Keri	kay-rhee	Kicking (Geri)
Keri Waza	kay-rhee wha-zah	Kicking techniques
Kiba Dachi	key-bah dah-chee	Horse stance
Kihon Ippon Kumite	key-hone ee-pon koo-me-teh	Basic one-step sparring
Kime	key-may	Focus
Kizami Zuki	key-zah-me zoo-key	Leading hand punch
Kokutsu Dachi	koh-koo-tsu dah-chee	Back stance
Koshi	ko-she	Ball of the foot
Kumite	koo-me-teh	Sparring
Kyu	quew	Rank below black belt
Ma-ai	mah-aye	Distancing
Mae	mah-eh	Front
Mae Geri	mah-eh geh-rhee	Front kick
Makiwara	mah-key-wha-rha	Striking board
Mawashi Empi	mah-wha-she en-pee	Round house elbow strike
Mawashi Geri	mah-wha-she geh-rhee	Round house kick
Mawashi Zuki	mah-wha-she zoo-key	Round house punch
Mawate	mah-wha-teh	Turn
Migi	me-ghee	Right
Mokuso	mo-koo-so	Meditation
Morote Sukui Uke	moh-row-teh sue-koo-ee oo-kay	Two-handed scooping block
Morote Uke	moh-row-teh oo-kay	Augmented forearm block
Musubi Dachi	moo-sue-be dah-chee	Informal attention stance, feet turned out
Nukite	noo-key-teh	Spear hand
Obi	o-bee	Belt-sash
Oi Zuki	oh-ee zoo-key	Stepping punch
Ryu	rhee-you	School (of karate)
Sanbon Kumite	san-bon koo-me-teh	Three-step sparring
Seiken	say-ken	Forefist
Seiza	say-zar	Kneeling position
Sempai	sem-pie	Senior
Sensei	sen-say	Teacher
Shizentai	she-zen-tah-ee	Natural position
Shuto	shoe-toe	Knife hand
Shuto Uchi	shoe-toe oo-chee	Knife hand strike
Shuto Uke	shoe-toe oo-kay	Knife hand block
Sokuto	sow-koo-toe	Edge of foot
Suki	sue-key	Opening
Tai Sabaki	tar-ee sah-bah-kee	Body shifting
Teisho	tay-show	Palm heel
Teisho Uchi	tay-show oo-chee	Palm heel strike
Teisho Uke	tay-show oo-kay	Palm heel block
Uchi	oo-chee	Strike
Uchi Uke	oo-chee oo-kay	Inside block
Uchi Waza	oo-chee wah-zah	Striking techniques
Ude	oo-day	Forearm
Ude Uke	oo-day oo-kay	Outside block
Uke	oo-kay	Block
Uraken Uchi	oo-rah-ken	Back fist strike
Ushiro Geri	oo-she-row geh-rhee	Back kick
Wan	wahn	Arm
Yame	yah-may	Stop/finish
Yoi	yoy	Ready stance
Yoko	yoh-koh	Side
Yoko Geri	yoh-koh geh-rhee	Side thrust kick
Zen	zen	Form of Buddhism based on meditation
Zenkutsu Dachi	zen-koo-tsue dah-chee	Front Stance
Zuki	zoo-key	Punch

Resources

Useful Contacts

If you are looking for a reputable club to train at, the internet is a very useful source of information. There are numerous sites for JKA-affiliated organizations, and most contain links listing specific club addresses, so you should be able to find one near to where you live. A few useful websites are listed below, along with the contact details for the JKA Headquarters in Tokyo.

JAPAN KARATE ASSOCIATION HEADQUARTERS
16–2, Ebisu-Nishi
Shibuya-Ku
Tokyo 150 Japan
Tel: (03) 3476-4611
Fax: (03) 3476-0322
e-mail: jka@red.an.egg.or.jp

KARATE UNION OF GREAT BRITAIN
www.kugb.org
Lists clubs by area throughout Great Britain.

JKA BOSTON
www.jkaboston.com
Contains details for clubs throught the United States.

ISKF CLUB INDEX
www.iskf.com/clubindex/index.htm
Plenty of club details for the United States and Canada, plus some useful contact details for Australia in the 'World' category.

Further Reading

Dynamic Karate, M. Nakayama. Kodansha, 1987.
The master text, with every technique explained in minute detail by the late chief instructor of the JKA. First published in 1966, this is an accepted masterpiece and should be on every karate-ka's bookshelf – no matter what their style.

Karate-Do: My Way of Life, Gichin Funakoshi. Kodansha, 1981.
The founder of modern karate's life story – an inspiration to all.

Moving Zen, C. W. Nicol. Paul H. Crompton, 1989.
The story of a man's journey to Japan to learn karate, and his adventures along the path to black belt. A must for any followers of Shotokan karate. The author trains with some of karate's legends. An inspiring and moving right of passage.

Zen in the Martial Arts, Joe Hyams. Bantam Books, 1982.
Anecdotes from a lifelong martial artist who relates the study of Budo to everyday life. Full of insight – anyone who has suffered the highs and lows of training will appreciate this book.

Index

Author's Acknowledgements

This book owes its life to many people. So here goes. To Dr Pam Spurr, for telling me I could do it. To Liz Wheeler, for believing me when I said I could do it. To Collette, Jason and Lauren, for working so hard modelling for the book. To Laura Wickenden, who is not only a fantastic photographer, but a lovely lady as well. To Tess, for the way she has slaved over every word I have written but always kept her sense of humour. To Hayley, for her superb layouts, snazzy jumpers and keeping me in line. To Jacqueline, for all her support, giving me time to write, and reading text while looking after five children – a remarkable feat, a remarkable lady. And lastly, the triplets – Max, Saskia and Sophia – who, through keeping me awake night after night, gave me the opportunity to sit and write. I thank you all. I couldn't have done it without you.

EDDISON·SADD EDITIONS

Commissioning Editor	Liz Wheeler
Senior Editor	Tessa Monina
Proofreader	Nikky Twyman
Indexer	Dorothy Frame
Art Director	Elaine Partington
Art Editor	Hayley Cove
Mac Designer	Brazzle Atkins
Production	Karyn Claridge and Charles James
Picture Researcher	Diana Morris
Map Illustrator	Lorraine Harrison
Japanese Translator	Anne Wolfson
Calligraphy	Ruth Rowland
Models	Kevin Healy, Jacqueline Healy, Lauren Healy, Collette Whiteman and Jason Ramsay

Picture credits: Corbis: Kevin R. Morris – 9; Michael S. Yamashita – 14–15; Jerome Prevost/TempSport – 127.

Eddison Sadd would like to thank Shogun International, London, for supplying the karate gi used in photography. Thanks also to Weld Enterprises Ltd, Lulworth Estate, Dorset, for permission for location photography. And special thanks to Phillip Southgate for all his help.